Endurance

Heroic Journeys in Ireland

DERMOT SOMERS

Born in Roscommon, Dermot Somers is a mountaineer, writer, Gaelic scholar, broadcaster and TV presenter. He has written and presented many programmes for television on wild landscape, culture, travel and adventure. His books include two works of fiction: *Mountains and Other Ghosts* (1990), the award-winning short-story collection, *At the Rising of the Moon* (1994), and his first book in Irish, also an award-winner, *Rince ar na Ballaí* (2002). A member of the successful Irish Everest Expedition 1993, Dermot's love of mountains and travel has taken him to wild places in Ireland, Scotland, the Alps, the Andes, the Himalayas, the Sahara and the Arctic tundra. He continues to make numerous climbing and trekking trips, combining his sense of the outdoors with a love of history, language and remote culture.

Endurance

HEROIC JOURNEYS IN IRELAND

DERMOT SOMERS

THE O'BRIEN PRESS
DUBLIN

First published 2005 by The O'Brien Press Ltd.,
20 Victoria Road, Dublin 6,
Ireland.
Tel: +353 1 4923333; Fax: +353 1 4922777
E-mail: books@obrien.ie
Website: www.obrien.ie

ISBN: 0-86278-797-1

British Library Cataloguing-in-Publication Data
Somers, Dermot
Endurance : heroic journeys in Ireland
1.Heroes - Ireland - History
2.Mythology, Irish
3.Ireland - History
4.Ireland - Folklore
1.Title
941.5

1 2 3 4 5 6 7 8
05 06 07 08

Typesetting, editing, layout and design: The O'Brien Press Ltd
Maps: Anú Design
Cover images: Anú Design, The Irish Image Collection, and the author
Printing: MPG Books Ltd

CONTENTS

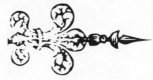

Introduction

We Irish have done more than our share of coming and going. One of our oldest traditions relates the arrival of Noah's granddaughter, Ceasair, on our shores. A few days before the Flood, she landed with three men and fifty women. The men were overwhelmed and the group died out. Others followed and got the balance right. Today, the Irish diaspora reaches to the furthest corners of the Earth.

Traditionally, the Gaelic bards and historians rooted us deep in the Old Testament and traced our ancestors on a biblical trek from the Black Sea to Spain and then northwards to colonise this island. The facts are far less certain. Our language itself, Indo-European in origin, has a transcontinental record. While the European Celts who brought the language did not actually *invade* Ireland, their culture soon came to dominate the earlier inhabitants, a process that began *c.*300 BC.

The journeys selected here are a personal choice, based on the linkage of story and landscape; they are confined within the island of Ireland itself. Voyagers, such as St Brendan and St Colmcille, who put to sea, have been allowed to sail away unhindered. The journeys here range from the myth of prehistory to events in the early seventeenth century, on the brink of modern Ireland. All of the accounts are founded on the realities of the countryside and the culture of their time, from the Iron Age to the post-Elizabethan era. The landscape throughout reflects the author's fascination with Gaelic Ireland. That tribal society had its own sophisticated laws and manners and, regrettably, its own self-obsessed elite. Before it fell into the hands of surveyors and cartographers, Gaelic Ireland was a country mapped out in poem and place name, measured in genealogy and myth. To walk the landscape (as the *aes dána*, the learned classes, constantly did) was a narrative act in itself.

Although they span fifteen hundred years, all the journeys recounted here traverse a thinly populated landscape, devoid of modern roads or transport. Rivers, bogs and mountains, and extremes of weather add rigour to the travel and lend a heroic dimension to the kings, queens, saints, scholars and fugitives involved. The tradition of the wandering bard might be thought of as filling the spaces between the lines.

THE JOURNEYS

Ireland's epic, Táin Bó Cuailnge, the Cattle-raid of Cooley, describes a military expedition that reflects the transition from European Celt to Irish warrior. Queen Medb's cross-country journey two thousand years ago, from Connacht to northeast Ulster, is outlined by its ancient narrators with a clarity that would enable it to be faithfully re-enacted tomorrow. It offers a virtual guidebook to Iron Age travel in Ireland. Charged with sexual tension, laced with humour and intrigue, the Táin contains characters that are timeless. On a political level, analysis of the story reveals that its underlying enmities still poison the Ireland of today.

The same impression of a hardy, mobile people is reflected in the tradition of the Fianna. These were pre-Christian warriors striding through a detailed country that has always seemed familiar to its inhabitants, because stories were as much part of the landscape as was the weather.

In folk memory, monks, missionaries and saints were given powers of excursion similar to those of the Fianna, for-ever dashing off to remote places until they spilled off the island itself for want of space, fetching up as far afield as Iceland and the Alps. Within Ireland itself, missionary travel is monopolised by legends of St Patrick. However, a medie-val text, *Acallamh na Seanórach* (*Discourse of the Elders*), exists, in which the saint's journey is fused with that of a pagan war-rior, and both traditions are asserted in graphic detail.

One of the most inspiring journeys of all in the long tradi-tion of the travelling monk is comparatively recent. Not a myth at all, it was undertaken by Michael O'Clery, Franciscan brother and chief of the Four Masters, who returned in 1626 to a homeland largely stripped of monasteries and monks. His exhaustive journeys of research, culminating in the Annals of the Four Masters, reveal a powerful sense of spiritual and intellectual quest, which preserved much ancient lore and learning that would otherwise have been lost.

Several dramatic journeys in the Irish landscape involved escape-attempts. Virtually everything previously written about the flight of Red Hugh O'Donnell and Art O'Neill from Dublin Castle in 1592 has added to the confusion surrounding the famous prison-break. The so-called 'princes of the north' and their historical context are clarified here in a sustained attempt to separate romantic illusion from fact and possibility. Mountain experience and a close reading of the landscape are brought to bear on the winter's journey of the fugitives through the Wicklow hills, where they succumbed to exposure and frostbite.

While many are aware of the presence of Don Francisco de Cuéllar in Elizabethan Ireland after the loss of his Armada ship on the Sligo coast in 1588, the Spanish captain's background, his character and his seven-month journey throughout the north of Ireland are not well-known. One of the features of his story, verified by alternative sources, was the unpredictability of the Irish response to the Spaniards, ranging from outright brutality to great generosity. It is fascinating to examine what this sea captain thought of the native Irish 'savage', writing, as he was, in a century when Spanish *conquistadores* were exterminating native peoples of South America (de Cuéllar had been there earlier in his career).

Other impressive journeys involved military conquest. A few decades before Brian Boru's truncated Circuit of Ireland

(1006), a northern king of the Uí Néill, called Muircheartach of the Leather Cloaks, marched clockwise with a thousand men around the entire country, in winter, taking hostages all the way. En route, he dispensed gifts among his allies and received tributes of food, including bacon, wheat and cheese from the Danes in Dublin (where a mysterious woman, close to his heart, came out to meet him).

Sixty years later, that northern ruler's descendants were riven with feuds, and a southern king – Brian Boru – was able to parade through their terrain, taking hostages from their headquarters at the *Grianán* of Aileach (in what today is Co. Donegal).

Challenging the traditional dynasty, the hard-travelling Brian Boru made a determined effort to impose national sovereignty on the unruly provinces of Ireland. Traditionally represented as a Circuit of Ireland, his journey is more aptly described as a Tour of the North.

 # PENANCE

Extraordinary journeys of penance have been recorded throughout Irish history. Leaving the truth aside, St Colmcille is believed to have quit Donegal for the Scottish island of Iona out of remorse over a battle he had caused. Having sworn never to view his homeland again, he swathed his face in cloth on his inevitable return. This impression of the sixth-century cleric, his eyes bandaged in cheesecloth, bumping into things, while former enemies hurled clods at him, is one of the eeriest images of the travelling Irish.

In the sixteenth century, Heneas MacNicaill made a pilgrimage around the most inaccessible of the holy sites, including Glendalough in Wicklow, Skellig Michael off the Kerry coast, Mount Brandon, Inis Mór of the Aran Islands, and the scree-ridden Croagh Patrick in Co. Mayo. It must have been a harrowing journey in 1543, not only because of the travelling conditions and the penitential locations visited, but also because Heneas was doing penance for the strangling of his own son – a dark shadow to trail at the best of times. We know nothing of the pilgrim though, apart from his crime and his itinerary and that echo of Virgil in his name.

Internecine strife was, however, a regular feature of Gaelic nobility, and if all who harmed family members in the pursuit of personal ambition had gone on pilgrimage, there would have been queues at the shrines.

❃ Farmers and Cattlemen

The endurance of the Irish race was affirmed in the early seventeenth century by Philip O'Sullivan, a Cork-born historian writing in Spain. He assured the whole world that the Irish were 'of elegant build … of great physical and intellectual vigour, highly skilled in warfare, and most tolerant of cold, heat, thirst and hunger.'

There is nothing to quarrel with in that surely, even if it contrasts with the opinion of his contemporary, Peter Lombard, who described the Irish as 'all too indolent, whence they are all the more prone to lapse into lovemaking and carousing.' Lombard should have known; he was Archbishop of Armagh. If both descriptions are true, we are, at least, a well-rounded race.

Whether the Irish, in general, really were as tough and rugged as O'Sullivan asserts, is open to question. There is a romantic impression that we were a semi-nomadic society, freewheeling across the hillsides for centuries, our herds (and those robbed from our neighbours) stampeding before us. In fact, we tended instead towards a fixed lifestyle, with settled homesteads within defined boundaries. Most people were rooted to the wrists and the ankles in the land itself, in the struggle for subsistence.

Even when Gaelic overlords were displaced during the Plantations of the sixteenth and seventeenth centuries, the smallholders were often retained by successive landlords because tenants of any kind were a valuable commodity.

Where upland pasture existed, animals were taken there for grazing during the summer months, by herders who remained with them in the hills. A limited form of transhumance, this tradition survived to the verge of the twentieth century as 'boolying' (*buailteachas* – summer grazing). The traces of rough stone huts belonging to this practice are still recognisable on the hillsides. Such grazing traditions did not involve major tribal movements into the hills, unless under attack, as in the case of Tadhg MacClancy, a Leitrim chieftain whose castle at Rosclogher was besieged by the English during Francisco de Cuéllar's visit.

The average individual throughout our history may have been hardy but was certainly not of heroic stature or endurance, as health and diet were poor. Hunger was not unusual, particularly in times of strife, or bad weather, or both. Food was seasonal, as was dairy produce, since cows have a dry season and are not productive in poor conditions. The large-scale dependence on cattle made subsistence unreliable, and famine was not uncommon.

However, battles were less frequent and less bloody than is often imagined, and the numbers involved were generally small because of the problems and expense of fielding an army from a sparse population, more productively occupied with agriculture.

✳ FOOT SOLDIERS AND HORSEBOYS

Much of the tradition of hardihood comes from the memory of legendary warriors and the undoubted feats of the 'kerns' who replaced them in historical times. Kerns were the Irish foot soldiers whose weapons for a thousand years were the short spear and the sword – until the odd musket fell into their hands in the sixteenth century. The kern (*ceithearnach*: member of a war band), formed the infantry of the Irish, and the records of forced marches that punctuate our history are greatly to their credit. Such men marched up to fifty miles a day on O'Donnell's lightning raids deep into the heart of Connacht from Donegal and Sligo during the Nine Years' War, their forays reaching as far south as Co. Clare. They tramped south with Hugh O'Neill, in winter, from Ulster to the Battle of Kinsale, and, after that bitter defeat, they jogged back home again, dying by the score on the way.

The 'rakehell horse-boyes', as the grooms of the Irish horsemen were termed by the poet Spenser, were equally hardened. Commonly barefoot, they accompanied professional soldiers into battle, taking care of their equipment and spare horses, and doubtless lending a violent hand when required. Their masters were often 'gallowglasses' of Scottish origin (*gall óglaigh*: foreign warriors).

Kerns and horseboys, many of them from Connacht, survived O'Sullivan Beare's famished march from west Cork in 1602–3, while the civilian refugees accompanying the march suffered appalling privations. They are described as feeding on watercress and foraging for leaves and wild roots.

 # FAMINE FOOD

The most common famine food in Ireland was *praiseach* or charlock, a tall, yellow-flowered weed, related to the cabbage family. Also known as cornweed and wild kale, it was inclined to turn the skin yellow. Its leaves were shredded and boiled into a disagreeable soup. The buds were eaten like a kind of broccoli. *Praiseach* was not available during the winter.[1]

Nettles too were widely used. They grow well on disturbed soil and were thought to be at their best in graveyards.

Chickweed, a common trailing plant, could be eaten all year round, boiled or raw. The root of the common thistle was boiled or fried. It could also be pounded into flour. The wild parsnip was found in winter, and the root of the versatile dandelion was edible throughout the year.

 # ROADS AND FORDS

The idea of roads in the ancient Irish landscape carries with it a cloud of confusion, or of magic, depending on the perspective. Because early history became legend so long ago, and because no one laid down a national road-system, as the

Romans and the Incas did elsewhere, the plain facts became creatively obscure. A notion developed of Five Great Roads radiating out from Tara (seat of the so-called High Kings in Meath) to the provinces. They were called *Slí Mhór, Slí Dhála, Slí Mhidluachra, Slí Assail, Slí Chualann.* These are more likely to have been general routes with complex local strands, rather than specific highways. They were reputed to have come into existence, mysteriously, AD 123, on the birth of Conn Céadchathach (Conn of the Hundred Battles), the founder of Connacht. That great king is an invention of legend, and his royal roads are equally lacking in foundation.

There is, however, no mystery in the real origin of roads. They begin as tracks, and the process may be observed in any remote part of the world today where a population encroaches on wild landscape. Left to themselves, cattle and sheep will work out the driest route between any two points. If a track is kept out of the swampy bottoms, as any farmer will ensure that it is, a bit of transverse drainage will go a long way towards the illusion of a road. All that is required is a channel cut at regular intervals, allowing water to run off to one side. Paving is achieved by dropping stones into muddy sections. The surface must not be a hazard to hooves. Locals have a reflexive skill with their native stone. They can also be put to digging ditches. For centuries, the Irish used slave labour extensively – often prisoners of war – and it is reasonable to imagine early chain-gangs clearing roads.

There is very little in the way of transport and travel that cannot be achieved by a gang of hardy men with a few pack animals. The use of sticks, kicks and stones may be observed today among drivers of every animal, from the donkey to the yak, crossing the roughest terrain in the world. A pack animal

1 KIDNAP AND JAILBREAK

Red Hugh O'Donnell (1587–92)

Everyone enjoys a jailbreak – preferably in the distance. We hope that we would be handy with files and ropes ourselves if the need arose.

Red Hugh O'Donnell broke out of prison twice, and made two wild dashes over the winter mountains before he was twenty. His flight from Dublin to Wicklow in 1592 is the most celebrated mountain journey in Irish history. The tale is fundamentally sound, but there are many versions. How much of what we believe is true? Where does the story come from, and, strange as the question sounds, where does the story go?

Red Hugh O'Donnell (*c.*1573–1602) was the son of a sixteenth-century lord of Tír Chonaill, more or less Co.

Donegal today. His mother was the chieftain's second wife, and Red Hugh was several decimal points away from the title. There were at least four other challengers among his kinsmen. Before he was fifteen, a marriage was arranged for him with the neighbouring lordship, the O'Neills of Tír Eoghain. Unity breaking out in Ulster alarmed Queen Elizabeth I's lord deputy in Dublin. He knew that Gaelic harmony could only be subversive.

Fostered out among the lesser chieftains, Red Hugh had taken part in his first feuding raid at the age of twelve, riding with an O'Gallagher against the O'Rourkes of Breifne. He spent about three years with MacSweeney Doe whose blocky thug of a castle still hunches at the head of Sheephaven Bay in the far north of Tír Chonaill, its wall-eyed stare fixed on the estuary.

The main O'Donnell castle, his father's home, stood at the mouth of the River Eske in the crook of Donegal Bay. Once described as 'the largest and strongest fortress in all of Ireland', it has recently been restored. Jostled by the hotels and shops of Donegal town, it stands its ground by grumpy force of character.

Red Hugh's mother, Iníon Dubh, was a 'great bringer in of Scots' by reputation. It seemed she had only to whistle and mercenaries came pouring into Donegal. Red Hugh shot up the list of succession when she took a violent hand, shortening the odds with Shakespearean efficiency.

O'Donnell's short life hinged repeatedly on dramatic journeys. He lived hard, he died young, and his biographer sainted him. His life story was grafted, complete, into the Annals of the Four Masters, a record of Irish history compiled a generation after his death. Though his adventures caught the public imagination down the centuries, he never quite earned his reputation as the key rebel of his time. That role belongs to his ally and in-law, Hugh O'Neill, Earl of Tyrone.

Lughaidh Ó Cléirigh, who wrote *Beatha Aodha Ruaidh Uí Dhomhnaill*, the 'Life of Red Hugh O'Donnell', was a contemporary. His family had been historians to the O'Donnells for hundreds of years. The political and military judgements are gloriously skewed in favour of the O'Donnells by the house historian, but the 'Life' does not stand entirely on trust. There are other sources: fat mirrors and thin mirrors, all flawed, but each giving clues to the others' distortions.

Red Hugh was snapped up by the English as a hostage at the age of fourteen. His father had reneged on a deal to hand over a younger son as a pledge, a human guarantee, and to pay an annual rent of cattle to the lord deputy in Dublin. The status of a pledge varied between house-guest, hostage and abject prisoner. O'Donnell was destined for the third category.

KIDNAP

On 29 September 1587, a vessel arrived in Lough Swilly, a long inlet on the northeast coast of Tír Chonaill. The ship has been identified as the Matthew, and the captain was Nicholas Barnes of Dublin.1 He would earn £100 for the job. In the bitter words of the 'Life' by Ó Cléirigh, 'A black-prowed deceiving ship was equipped in Dublin with a malevolent, warlike crew ….'

Disguised as a trading vessel, the ship anchored in Lough

Swilly well out in the current, opposite an O'Sweeney castle at Rathmullan. The crew went ashore, posing as merchants in wine and beer. The people of the castle, the Fanad Sweeneys, had priority and got drunk first. Soon the entire neighbourhood followed suit.

The young Red Hugh O'Donnell was in the area with some companions, visiting Rathmullan Castle. Hospitality being a prime virtue, MacSweeney Fanad sent out for more drink to impress his guests. But stocks had run dry and the merchants had returned to the ship. They invited MacSweeney to bring his visitors on board, where they might dip into a private supply.

Launching a small boat that lay on the shore, the Donegal men rowed themselves out into the bay. They can almost be heard smacking their lips in the process, or maybe it's just the splash of keen oars. As if to increase the irony, the crew allowed aboard only the prisoners they particularly wanted, including Red Hugh and a couple of prime young nobles – this according to Ó Cléirigh in the 'Life'. No doubt, the re-jects felt hard done by at first. When the plot was revealed, their relief at having escaped must have been clouded by the implication that they were not worth capturing.

There was nothing random about the raid. Perrott, Queen Elizabeth's lord deputy, had earlier proposed the capture of the O'Donnell chieftain, his wife and their son, Red Hugh, 'by sending them a boat with wines'. The Irish were known to be particularly fond of sack, the sweet wine associated with Falstaff and Prince Hal.

Ó Cléirigh is tightlipped in the 'Life', protecting local reputations. An account by the historian, Philip O'Sullivan, written a few years later, rips the curtain aside. He says that

❧ The Commentators

The O'Clery family (Uí Cléirigh) were hereditary historians to the O'Donnell chieftains of Donegal from the fourteenth to the early seventeenth century.

Lughaidh Ó Cléirigh, born *c.*1580, a contemporary of Red Hugh O'Donnell, was the last to perform the function. His cousin, Mícheál was chief of the Four Masters (See Chapter 7) and Lughaidh himself is often thought, wrongly, to have been one of the famous annalists. However, the entire text of his *Beatha Aodha Ruaidh Uí Dhomhnaill*, the Life of Red Hugh O'Donnell, was incorporated into the Annals as an account of the Nine Years' War. Lughaidh, a poet, was an instigator of the notorious war of words between the northern and the southern poets, *Iomarbhágh na bhFileadh*, the Contention of the Bards.

Philip O'Sullivan Beare was born *c.*1590 in west Cork. A nephew of Donal Cam O'Sullivan, chieftain of Beare, he was sent to Spain while still a child as a pledge to Philip III in return for aid to the O'Sullivans. He went on to have a career in the Spanish Navy and to become a writer and 'historian'.

His best known work is *Historiae Catholicae Iberniae Compendium*, (Irish Catholic History), written in Latin and published in 1621. It includes an account of Red Hugh O'Donnell's capture and escape.

A passionate exile, 'Don Philippo' (as the Spaniards called him) wore his heart on his sleeve and it dripped constantly on to the page. He couldn't resist making a good story better – which is a virtue in a novelist, a flaw in a historian.

both MacSweeney Doe and MacSweeney Fanad were on board, along with a very senior O'Gallagher. Frantic bartering ensued. MacSweeney Fanad traded his son, Dónal Gorm, as a hostage, and was released. O'Gallagher traded a nephew. A peasant boy was sent aboard dressed as the son of MacSweeney Doe, and that cunning chieftain was allowed to leave. On their arrival in Dublin, the lord deputy is said to have released the young peasant immediately.

Rathmullan, a holiday destination, enjoys a liberal reputation today, catering for Donegal and Derry. Licensing laws are still flexible. Other dramatic events have been witnessed there, including the 'Flight of the Earls', when Hugh O'Neill and other Gaelic leaders abandoned Ulster to go into exile in 1607.

During the First World War, large sections of the British fleet were anchored in Lough Swilly, and Admiral Jellicoe had a long-term suite in Rathmullan Hotel, close to the point where the *Matthew* anchored over three hundred years before.

# PRISON

So began O'Donnell's first dramatic journey – probably with violence; surely with embarrassment; more than likely with a hangover. The *Matthew* sailed north to Malin Head, east along the Antrim coast, through Rathlin Sound and south by Belfast Lough, past the Mournes and Dundalk Bay, past the mouth of the Boyne, further south to Howth and finally into Dublin Bay. The capture of Red Hugh had been such a success that there was some unofficial talk of kidnapping others by similar means and of possibly locking up his parents when they visited Dublin at a later date. Recorded in state papers, these schemes create an image of the Irish wallowing like slugs in beer-traps.

The prison cells of Dublin Castle reeked of affliction in the time of Red Hugh, when there are reported to have been twenty hostages, three priests and a bishop held. In the words of Ó Cléirigh, written with a lump in his ink, they passed the days and nights 'lamenting the insufferable hardships and relating the great cruelty that was inflicted on them ….' Confinement within the walls of an alien capital can only have been bitter for Red Hugh, an impetuous youth with the Atlantic in his nostrils. But there were plenty of O'Donnells pleased to see him banged up and out of competition for the title. In his absence, his mother buttressed her husband's waning power. Thanks to her, several of Red Hugh's rivals passed away violently.

For the first three and a quarter years of his captivity (September 1587–January 1591), the prisoner was kept in a tower flanking the main entrance to the Castle – not the Bermingham Tower, as frequently claimed. He was held in one of the twin towers of the Main Gate, and the details of the breakout confirm this. Today, the elegant Bedford Tower stands on top of that original prison block, which has disappeared into Castle Hall. His quarters overlooked the portcullis and drawbridge. For external company, he had the heads of executed prisoners extended on poles, in honour of which these famous lines were written by Richard Stanyhurst:

> *Those trunkless heads do plainly show each rebel's fatal end*
> *And what a heinous crime it is, the Queen for to offend.*

The details of the gate-tower with its fringe of skulls are clearly visible in an illustration by John Derricke, done in 1581, showing the lord deputy of the time riding out of Dublin Castle. O'Donnell's first breakout a decade later could have been masterminded using only this drawing. It is often cropped in print, but the full illustration shows the lower windows of the twin gate-towers as narrow slits, with a larger

❧ *Ropework*

With a very long rope, *téittrefedh rofhoda*, they lowered themselves down to the drawbridge and blockaded the Castle door from the outside with a balk of timber wedged through its external ring.   Ó CLÉIRIGH IN THE 'LIFE'.

People are forever swarming up and down ropes in books, but it's not that easy, in fact. To descend a rope, hand over hand, is a precarious business – especially the initial moves where the rope is running over the edge of a windowsill, pinning the fingers against the stone. The sailor's trick of trapping the rope between the feet is plausible enough with a thick nautical rope, hawser-laid. However, such a rope is unlikely to have been smuggled in to the prisoners or concealed within. If a thick rope had been hauled up on a string from the drawbridge, as some have imagined, there would be no reason for the 'Life' to conceal the fact. The idea of a thick rope is contradicted by the word Ó Cléirigh uses, *suainemhnaibh*, which, although it can mean a rope, is more likely to refer to a thin cord.

One way to descend a slender rope or cord is to tie big knots in it for handholds, or even loops for the hands and feet, although that would use up an enormous amount of rope. John O'Donovan, translating an account of the escape from the Annals of the Four Masters, favours the notion of loops in the rope. References from documents of the day mention a type of silk called 'sarsnet', from which a line could be made.

There is one other way to descend a slender rope and that is by means of a *classic abseil*: passing the rope backwards between the legs, up around the hip, diagonally across the chest, over the shoulder and down across the back to wrap around the wrist where it is released slowly for maximum friction. This was a traditional method of descent practised by climbers, rarely used now, for reasons of safety and comfort. Rope-burns were common. Inexpertly used, it added a transverse cleavage to the buttocks.

window on the upper floor, overlooking the drawbridge. It can only have been through this window, or the hidden one in the left-hand tower, that Red Hugh and a number of his companions escaped for the first time at the end of winter 1591.

The escape is said to have occurred early in the night. It is hard to imagine that a line of men scuttling down a rope on the front wall of the Castle would not have been spotted and the alarm raised, since the drawbridge was faced by a street and a row of houses. The fact that the guard on the Castle Gate was absent and that the prisoners had a rope means that money was involved. Contemporary papers reveal the constant bribery of officials by Hugh O'Neill, Earl of Tyrone, and also the offer of very large sums by O'Donnell's parents. Red Hugh's father handed over a group of shipwrecked sailors from the Spanish Armada in an attempt to prise the hostage loose. The Spaniards were hanged by the lord deputy.

Several prisoners escaped with O'Donnell. They are assumed to have been the other victims of the Rathmullan kidnap. Historical fiction, in need of colour on a winter's night, has made great play of Dónal Gorm's blue eyes and O'Donnell's red hair. The escape was an organised conspiracy, not a random breakout. According to the 'Life', there was a young man waiting with a pair of swords, one of which Red Hugh handed to Art Kavanagh to cover the rear. Kavanagh was a member of a famous fighting family, drafted in for the purpose. The road to the south was guarded by St Nicholas' Gate, which had a double-tower and portcullis. It was open and the fugitives slipped through.

They were on their way to Glenmalure, in present-day Wicklow, mountain stronghold of Fiach MacHugh O'Byrne, who continued to defy the Crown despite his proximity to

Dublin. O'Byrne had the status of a guerrilla chieftain, and his area was a haven for rebels and fugitives.

Although Glenmalure itself was nearly thirty miles (fifty kilometres) away, the security of the foothills lay within a couple of hours' reach. Beyond the walls of the city, the fugitives leaped over ditches, gardens and walls, avoiding the roads. Ó Cléirigh indulges in a gleeful flashback, relishing the scene after the fugitives have fled, as if he had witnessed it himself. Discovering the escape, the guards rushed to the castle-door where they were blocked by the wooden cross-piece in the chain. They roused the people in the houses opposite the gate. The timber was removed, and a great crowd surged in pursuit.

❋ FUGITIVES

The escape was to be no more than a painful rehearsal. Ó Cléirigh says that they headed for the mountain slope lying directly south. 'The mountain is long and very wide,' he adds. The route-description is equally succinct: 'travelling all night, they crossed the red mountain.' If modern guidebooks took the hint, they might restore the adventure to walking.

Sliabh Ruadh, the Red Mountain, traditionally meant the Dublin and Wicklow mountains lumped together. Events indicate that the fugitives were probably on the eastern (seaward) slopes of the hills. The guide would have avoided roadblocks on the lower routes where horsemen were already stumbling and cursing southwards. It is too easy to assume that the people of the hillsides would automatically assist the escape. What allegiance did a Leinster peasant owe to a fugitive aristocrat from Donegal?

There is a local tradition that O'Donnell crossed Three Rock Mountain during both of his escapes, and that this mountain, overlooking south Dublin, was actually *Sliabh Rua*. The repetition of the rumour down the centuries has fed back into the tradition itself and reinforced it. While the summit of Three Rock is most unlikely, it is reasonable to speculate that the fugitives were led through that general area – over the plateau formed by Three Rock, Killakee and Prince William's Seat, and into either the Glencullen or the Glencree valley towards Enniskerry. One thing is certain: the teenaged Red Hugh would not have had the faintest notion of where he was from the moment he plunged into the wet darkness beyond Dublin.

Most commentators, however, have opted for a romantic passage straight and true among the high mountains, via Lough Bray and the Sally Gap towards Glendalough.[2] This is the line of the Military Road across the upland bogs. That road would not be built, however, until Red Hugh was dead and buried for a couple of centuries. The grazing tracks that preceded parts of it across the blanket bogs would have been a highly improbable route to have taken on a black winter's night of driving rain in January 1591 – especially for a group weakened by years in Dublin Castle.

The blankness of a mountain bog in winter darkness has to be experienced to be understood. The kind of foul weather that might conceal an escape from Dublin Castle is the very weather that would make a night traverse via Lough Bray and the Sally Gap impossible, centuries before any road existed. An influential account, written by Standish O'Grady in 1897, has the guide crouching at times to examine the ground for his whereabouts; at other points, he takes his bearings from the faint outline of the hills, or from the roar of rushing torrents. This romantic notion was inspired by the literature of Indian trackers that had become popular in frontier America at the time. Art Kavanagh, presumed to be the guide, picks his way unerringly through the night 'by the west side of Luggala, by Lough Dan and over the spurs of Mullaghcleevaun and Tonelagee ....'

It is unlikely that the writer of such a claim ever floundered in an upland bog on a winter's night. Without moon or stars. Without map, compass, raincoat, torch or hot soup. Without the faintest trace of a road, the beam of a headlight, or the glow of a village on the underbelly of a cloud. Visibility in such conditions is nil. Surely, after the hurdle of the first plateau was crossed, the fugitives were lower down, on the eastern slopes of the hills, and not among the upper ridges and bogs at all.

Fit walkers who know where they are going travel at a comfortable average of three miles (five kilometres) per hour, and can maintain that speed over long distances. Speed decreases on uphill sections, where the rule of thumb adds to the flat time an extra one minute per ten metres of height gained. Fugitives move faster, of course, but it might be in short bursts, and it is hard to keep it up as an average – especially in winter darkness, virtually barefoot, on rugged terrain.

They might have covered around twenty miles in a six- to eight-hour push, putting them within range of today's Roundwood, Annamoe, Ashford, with a further ten miles to go to Glenmalure. This would assume that they were fit, knew where they were going in the dark and made no exhausting diversions. But they may well have been further back – towards Enniskerry. Red Hugh's white-skinned, slender feet, *a throighthe toinngheala tanaidhe*, were torn by the furze and the briars and the ruggedness of the mountain. His light shoes were shredded. They went into a dense wood to rest until dawn, according to the 'Life'.

In the morning, O'Donnell could not continue. Could not, or would not? As a family historian, Ó Cléirigh would never raise such a scruple. The rest of the party went on successfully to Glenmalure, and we know that the Crown lost several hostages in the escape. But Red Hugh, always impulsive, was under the impression that rescue was closer to hand than Glenmalure. Left in the woods with a small party, he sent for help to Phelim O'Toole of Castlekevin, near Annamoe.

The O'Tooles had had their own hostages in the tender care of the Crown. Phelim O'Toole is thought to have visited Red Hugh in prison where they promised to help each other should an occasion ever arise. Significantly, Phelim's sister, Róis, was married to O'Byrne, the rebel chieftain of Glenmalure. According to one account, she was visiting her brother in Annamoe as the crisis developed.

The O'Tooles were traditional rulers of Kildare and the Wicklow area, but their power would not survive the coming Nine Years' War, of which Red Hugh was a sharp presentiment.

 ## Betrayal

He should have kept on going, feet or no feet. O'Toole failed him, and handed him back to the Castle authorities. There were circumstances, of course. Phelim's arm was twisted by his family and by associates with Crown connections. Red

Hugh's presence in the area had immediately become known to spies. Tracker-dogs were already on his trail, *cona luirg for a fhoillecht*. Whether he got away with the connivance of the O'Tooles or was recaptured in their company, they would have been hopelessly compromised. So, they handed him over. A warrant was issued by the lord deputy for the arrest of Hugh Roe O'Donnell at Castlekevin. The date was 25 January 1591. While this act of betrayal could easily be seen as a Judas-reflex, it has not attracted the hate mail of history. We understand the nature of that kiss too well.

There is another reason why the O'Tooles of Castlekevin have never quite been accused of treachery. Phelim's sister, Róis, at home on a visit, is said to have proposed that the fugitive be held overnight, as if awaiting arrest. Meanwhile, her husband, Fiach MacHugh O'Byrne, would raid the castle and carry Red Hugh away to Glenmalure before the soldiers arrived. O'Byrne, the outlaw, had nothing further to lose by enraging the English, while the O'Tooles could claim innocence of treachery to either side. If ever a plan deserved to succeed, that one did. The plot, stranger than fiction, was reported by Philip O'Sullivan, writing in Spain a generation later. According to him, it rained so heavily during the night that the rivers flooded and Fiach MacHugh O'Byrne could not get out of Glenmalure to raid Castlekevin before the English arrived. O'Sullivan, however, was an enthusiastic embellisher.

 # MANACLES

So, the rehearsal was over and O'Donnell was back in prison – in irons, this time. The fact that wiser companions had escaped must have been an unbearable echo of Rathmullan.

Ó Cléirigh resorts to stylised rhetoric to convey the grief of the Gaels: 'There came a great gloom over the Irish ... and the hearts of their heroes were weakened on hearing that news. There were many princesses and great ladies and beautiful, white-breasted maidens grieving and lamenting on his behalf.'

However, it was inevitable that O'Donnell would escape a second time from Dublin Castle, as if he had the appointment with destiny that storytelling demands. It would happen, not for narrative reasons, but because his allies were tirelessly plotting his escape, bombarding Crown officials with appeals and bribes. His installation as chief of the O'Donnells was important in the regional strategy of Hugh O'Neill, Earl of Tyrone. With the masterful O'Neill pulling strings, Red Hugh was going to get out, one way or the other. Whether he broke out, or was bought out, was the only question.

 ## SECOND ESCAPE

Breakout occurred a year later, on 24 December, when the guards were predictably drunk – a reversal of the roles at Rathmullan. The famous event developed a sense of nativity, or rebirth, as a result of the date. However, Christmas Eve 1591 became 5 January 1592, when the Gregorian calendar kicked in (wiping a week and a half off human existence, according to public opinion); so the annual re-enactment takes place on the eve of the Epiphany, with a night-walk from Dublin Castle to Glenmalure. This used to include kicking the Castle Gate at midnight before setting off on the journey – until one walker kicked the gate so hard that he broke his ankle and had to be carried home.

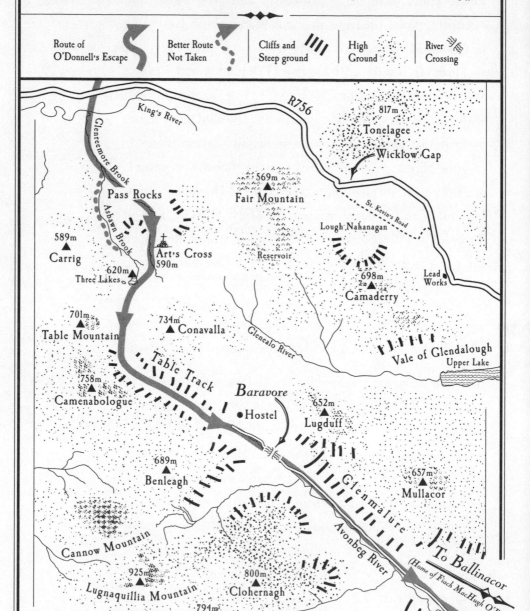

FINAL STAGE OF
O'DONNELL'S ROUTE TO GLENMALURE

(From King's River via Glenreemore Brook to Table Track, through Baravore and Drumgoff)

Route of O'Donnell's Escape | **Better Route Not Taken** | **Cliffs and Steep ground** | **High Ground** | **River Crossing**

R756

817m
Tonelagee

Wicklow Gap

King's River

St. Kevin's Road

569m
Fair Mountain

Lough Nahanagan

Glenreemore Brook

Pass Rocks

Ashawn Brook

Reservoir

698m
Camaderry

Lead Works

Art's Cross
590m

589m
Carrig

620m
Three Lakes

701m
Table Mountain

734m
Conavalla

Glenealo River

Vale of Glendalough
Upper Lake

Table Track

Baravore
•Hostel

652m
Lugduff

758m
Camenabologue

689m
Benleagh

657m
Mullacor

Glenmalure

Cannow Mountain

Avonbeg River

To Ballinacor

(Home of Fiach MacHugh O'Byrne)

925m
Lugnaquillia Mountain

800m
Clohernagh

794m
Corrigaslegaun

759m
Slievemaan

Drumgoff

❧ *Art O'Neill*

Art and Henry were the sons of Shane O'Neill, who had killed Hugh O'Neill's father in 1558 in pursuit of the title. Shane had also insulted Red Hugh's people by capturing a prominent O'Donnell and taking his wife for a mistress. Art O'Neill was an illegitimate son of this bizarre relationship. Henry O'Neill was one of only two legitimate sons from Shane's ten offspring by various women. Collectively known as the Mac Shanes, they had a strong claim on the O'Neill title, a claim aggressively pursued against Hugh O'Neill.

The annual night-march is not called after Red Hugh. It is known as 'The Art O'Neill Walk'. Art and his older brother, Henry, also escaped that night. Although it is well known that Hugh O'Neill, Earl of Tyrone, engineered the escape, it was not on account of these particular kinsmen, who were enemies of his. Contrary to the romantic impression of Art and Henry as princely youths, they were grown men, much older than Red Hugh. They had been imprisoned as pledges in Dublin Castle since 1585.

This time, the prisoners were in the formidable black tower, which is now the Garda Museum. With walls up to fifteen feet thick, it was far more secure than the prison block of the previous year. Surrounded at that time by a loop of the River Poddle, the tower formed the southeast corner of the Castle walls.[3]

The hostages were bound in iron fetters, which they managed to remove: *gattaid i ngeimhle díobh*, Ó Cléirigh says, as if they had taken off their shoes. Another account puts a noisy file in the hands of Red Hugh; it was a good thing the guards were drunk. Apparently the irons were inspected regularly for tampering, so there was only a single chance.

After the first escape, the lord deputy had replaced the prison superintendent with an elderly man called Maplesdene who is thought to have been seriously ill. This unfortunate man died less than forty-eight hours after the breakout. We don't know the circumstances, but a second-in-command was locked up 'with good store of irons'. Informed opinion suspects Sir William Fitzwilliam, the lord deputy, to have been the chief recipient of bribes, with Maplesdene as his pawn.

It was a foul winter's night. The prisoners lowered themselves down through a shaft in the walls of the tower. The Irish *fiailteach* is always translated as 'privy', and this is the word still used, even in modern guidebooks to Dublin Castle. There is no polite word for such a loathsome shaft, bearing in mind that it would not have been accessible if it had seemed a possible means of escape. There are hints, though, that it had been cleaned prior to the breakout. It is not hard to imagine what that might involve; the exit below was probably backed up and had to be cleared at intervals.

Ó Cléirigh mentions a rope again, without detail, but it is usually described as lengths of fabric knotted together. This is an interpretation of the 'sarsnet' or silk referred to in various references as material for making a line.[4]

Art O'Neill, who had been a long time in prison, was corpulent and thick-thighed – *collnach remhairshliastach*, in the blunt words of Ó Cléirigh. Presumably they left him until last, in case he got wedged in the shaft, or a knot slipped under his weight. Art is said to have been struck by a falling stone as he descended.

The sewer of Dublin Castle might well be thought of as the anal canal of imperialism. The moat was formed by the River Poddle, which cannot have been particularly wholesome either. They crossed it, climbed the opposite bank and found their guide. No spare clothing or footwear. The prisoners had left their heavy mantles in the tower. O'Donnell might have known better after his previous attempt. Either he was impulsive to the point of calamity (aspects of his later career back that up), or he believed the guide would have whatever was needed. Perhaps the shaft was so tight that they had to leave the garments behind, or maybe they could not have crossed the moat wearing heavy woollen cloaks.

Again, a pre-arranged escape, a conspiracy, with practical details poorly handled. Ó Cléirigh does not identify the reception party, but O'Sullivan's account has a young man called Edward Eustace involved. Four horses had been kept ready by Eustace for three nights, but friends had borrowed them that evening without permission. This man was Edward Fitzeustace, a young relative of the Viscount of Baltinglass who was the exiled leader of a rebellion with Fiach MacHugh O'Byrne. Even if Edward was involved in the plan, there is no suggestion that he accompanied the fugitives on foot when the horses disappeared. And yet, it can only be the mention of his name (by O'Sullivan only), combined with the location of Fitzeustace territory to the west of Glenmalure, that has led to the modern belief that the prisoners fled in that direction.

The 'Life' simply tells us that they crossed the slopes of Slieve Rua, 'where Red Hugh had come on his first escape'.

❧ *Fact or Fiction*

Ó Cléirigh, in the 'Life', clearly indicates a single guide – a trusty servant who had visited or attended them in the Castle and who 'met them face to face when it was necessary to be their guide'. Again, Ó Cléirigh, at firsthand, must have been better informed, and the graphic O'Sullivan must be less reliable. He gets the date of this second escape completely wrong, for example, setting it a few days after the first, instead of a year later. His errors and assumptions have had far-reaching effects on the story.

The Rev. Paul Walsh, in his modern commentary, accepts that there were two guides, one of them Edward Eustace, and that the escape route therefore went west through Fitzeustace territory – this despite the fact that the 'Life', which he was editing, says no such thing.

Sadly, the faithful guide does not merit identification. One thing is certain, though: east or west, he must have been a Wicklow mountain expert. This makes him almost certainly one of Fiach MacHugh O'Byrne's people. We know from contemporary reports that the Crown had spies in Glenmalure, while the rebels had their men in Dublin. The man who attended the prisoners and became their guide must have been one of those. The lord deputy pointed later to such a servant as the guide.

It was early in the night, the city gates not yet closed. They made their way through thronged streets and fled the city without being noticed. The fact that a group of men, having crawled through a toilet and waded through a sewer, roused no attention in the city implies that Dublin must have been hosting stag parties longer than we think.

Somewhere en route, they lost Henry O'Neill. It has been hinted that he may have separated from them deliberately, fearing a conspiracy against him. Henry is known to have made his way successfully home to Ulster, a very impressive feat given the hue and cry that had been raised. He was immediately locked up for the duration of the Nine Years' War by his kinsman, Hugh O'Neill, who liked to keep enemies under his own control, rather than in Dublin Castle where they might be used against him.

It did not pass without notice that Hugh O'Neill would have liked Art out of the way also. There were those who thought that Art had signed his own death warrant when he headed towards Glenmalure. No doubt they saw the 'Life', when it appeared, as a whitewash. The internecine politics of Gaelic Ireland were devious.

❧ *Night March*

The annual commemoration walk takes a route from Dublin Castle to Terenure, along the River Dodder to the Stone Cross and on to the Liffey at Ballysmuttan Bridge; on then past Sorrel Hill and Black Hill, over Billy Byrne's Gap to Glenbride; across the King's River and up Glenreemore on difficult ground to Art's Cross, past the Three Lakes on the plateau and down Table Track into Glenmalure. This route involves about twenty miles of road-walking, followed by nearly as much again across the hills. First put together by a group called *Na Fánaithe*, in 1952, the route has been chosen by the organisers as simply the safest modern one between two points, using mountain roads as far as possible. The route presumes entry into Glenmalure via the high western end of the narrow valley. It is based on assumptions that may be traced back to the mention of Edward Eustace and the missing horses.

❋ HYPOTHERMIA

Whichever direction they took, the fugitives were in trouble. The winter conditions, the darkness, the need for speed, their inadequate clothes and footwear – all induced the condition known today as exposure, or hypothermia: when the core-temperature of the body drops to a dangerous level, resulting in confusion and eventual collapse. Wet clothing, wind chill, fatigue and lack of high-energy food are the causes. A simple drop of 4°C in the core temperature causes disorientation; a drop of 7°C and the casualty falls into a coma; a loss of 10°C can be fatal. Simple exposure accounts for many mountain disasters. If the condition is not treated, it will kill. In one sense, mountains are utterly predictable: they will punish presumption. O'Donnell might have known what to expect, given his own previous fiasco and Art's physical condition.

As soon as they reached the winter foothills, the Ulstermen left politics behind and stumbled into the universal story of wilderness and escape. Their trials have occurred over and over throughout the world and will continue to afflict refugees, fugitives, hunters, traders and, of course, mountaineers. In the second half of the twentieth century, similar conditions have beset Tibetans fleeing through the mountains from Chinese rule. The Chinese imposed conditions in Tibet which were similar to those in Elizabethan Ireland.

'The night came on with drizzle and a downpour of rain and slippery snow…' *Gebidh an adhaigh for snidhe agus ferthain* …. Art O'Neill collapsed. Red Hugh and the guide hitched his arms across their shoulders and dragged the exhausted man along between them, 'over the pass of the mountain-plateau'.

This is unlikely. On rough terrain over any great distance, they would all have collapsed. The text is doing its duty by O'Donnell, reflecting him as a high-born hero of noble instinct. What else would be expected of a budding chief, or indeed of the tribal historian?

Victims of exposure become so confused that they can appear to be drunk, stumbling along, acting and speaking irrationally. Strength may surge and decline in erratic bursts. Immediate rest and re-warming is the only treatment. An inexperienced leader will often press on rather than look for shelter where the victim can be warmed between the bodies of his companions. The driving force is the single-minded need to reach a destination. Stronger members of the group may also be succumbing to exposure, their judgement eroded by rain and wind, and their decisions obstinate. Meanwhile, the body is protecting its core temperature by shutting off circulation to the extremities: hands and toes, ears, nose, cheeks. The initial pain of freezing fingers and toes – the warning system – has switched off, and the suffering has actually decreased. Frostbite does not require alpine or Himalayan conditions. With poor circulation, it can occur at a few degrees below zero, if the feet or hands are cold and wet for a long period.

Eventually the fugitives were forced to a halt; they could not drag Art any further. They took shelter under a high cliff-edge, *allbhruaich iomaird*, on the hillside. The guide continued on to Glenmalure in search of help. He must have been O'Byrne's man, because he knew the way forward on the mountain. He had already walked twenty-five miles or more, in winter, from Dublin Castle and might have had ten miles still to travel to Ballinacor, the home of O'Byrne. Then he had to return that distance with the rescue party, and back again afterwards to Glenmalure with the casualty. He was to traverse in and out of the valley three times on difficult terrain.

Whoever the man was, it was a terrible moment for him as he left his charges behind and forged ahead into the weather. Although existence had narrowed down to survival, he carried the symbolic force of their escape and its outcome. There is a powerful bond of responsibility on the strongest member of an afflicted group forced to go on alone. If he does not find help, if he returns too late, if he loses the way, if the weather worsens, there is no one but him to bear the consequence. A kind of guilty terror strikes the heart and grips it with the sense of what may happen in his absence. Everything depends on him.

The outcome has always fascinated hill-walkers and mountaineers, who have experienced the harshness of the landscape. The Wicklow hills are low and rounded, with a temperate climate, but winter can be vicious in a peculiarly local way. A summer hill becomes a winter mountain. On a bad night of biting winds and driving rain, when you have chosen to be out and gone too far to retreat, you strain into the weather, or tack across it on boggy slopes, while freezing rain stings the eyes and runs into the mouth and nostrils with every breath. There is a lack of definition in the landscape that causes confusion and loss of confidence – impossible to tell whether the ground ahead is rising or falling. Instinct is amputated. There can be nothing random involved, or you will go disastrously astray. You navigate by map and compass, with a head-torch. All of a sudden, a homely landscape has switched from comfort to conflict and the hostile element is not only the weather, but also the very ground itself. It is this power to change that fascinates.

They had almost made it. Travelling without cloaks – in tunics, linen shirts, tight trews and flimsy shoes – in rain, sleet, snow and wind, they had come within reach of Glenmalure, with an exhausted man, bloated by prison diet. In some accounts, there is a hint that the guide may have attempted to cover his companions with a layer of sods before leaving them. It sounds unlikely. There was an ancient practice, though, of making overnight shelters from hooped rods thatched with 'scraws' stripped from the surface of the ground. But this covering of the victims in a mantle of earth, true or not, suits a theme of death and resurrection, which is developing irresistibly at the core of the story. When the guide returned with help from Glenmalure, the two seemed to all intents and purposes to be frozen to death, shrouded in a mantle of hail, and blending into the surrounding earth. Ó Cléirigh's description of the savage scene almost conjures up a marble tomb in winter snow.

It is not difficult to fill in the silent details. Having started with an immersion in the moat, followed by a soaking night-march, the group is unlikely to have been moving fast the following day, given Art's condition. It could well have been afternoon when the guide left them, for that decision would have been postponed, hour by hour, until it was obvious at last that they would not reach Glenmalure together by the light of day.

Midwinter darkness closed in early and the guide would have had to allow himself enough time to cross difficult terrain if he were on the high western route, as popularly supposed. Then he had to descend into Glenmalure by what must have been a complex path. We are used to the valley now with a road and tracks opened up by lead-mining, farming and forestry, but it was a very different place in terms of access in 1592. It is possible that help did not arrive until the following day was advanced, as the rescuers would not have travelled without light to guide them over such terrain in winter weather – particularly with flooded streams and fords to cross.

In that case, the fugitives may have lain on the ground, virtually shoeless, for anything up to fifteen hours, while the wind blew and snow or hail fell intermittently. In those conditions, the sky sometimes clears and it freezes hard. Racing stars glitter between shreds of cloud. The air tastes like cold steel. Was Art dead by then? According to Ó Cléirigh, he died later, as the rescuers tried to revive him with ale. They may have been going through the motions. An exhausted victim of exposure would probably lose consciousness soon after he was lowered to the ground in freezing conditions. Art could have gone into a coma and died during the night. Hugh, attempting to shelter against the body, would have felt it turn stiff as a snowdrift beside him in a very short while.

He must have fought to stay awake himself as the numbness increased, knowing, as one instinctively does, that sleep might be irreversible. Reserves of willpower would have shrilled their alarm periodically. From time to time, in the darkness of the mind, there are voices, shouts, footsteps. That's how it works – a waking nightmare, the dream of death, jolting awake to the rhythm of soldiers' feet, the baying of bloodhounds yet again. He was in a coma when help arrived. Although he was forced back to consciousness, he would not have known what was happening to Art. The body turns entirely in upon itself, reflecting its own disaster.

When the rescue party reached them, the victims were shrouded in snow, the clothing frozen to their skin, and O'Donnell's feet were 'dead members without feeling owing to the swelling and blistering from the frost and snow'. They gave up the attempt to revive Art and buried him there on the hillside, wherever it was. What an eerie scene that must have been, with or without a moon. A rough excavation; or perhaps the body was simply heaped over with stones. They had to cover him, for there were wolves in Wicklow then.

ART'S CROSS

Today, a plaque in a niche under the Nye Rocks at the head of Glenreemore marks the spot where Art O'Neill is thought to have died, and there is a wooden cross high on the slopes above. Marked on the Ordnance Survey map of the plateau, Sheet 56, along with a scatter of little lakes, the cross provides an advanced exercise in navigation on a day or night of poor visibility. When it appears at last in a tunnel of mist, there is no sense of a real conclusion. It marks a supposition, floating between calendars, between memory and myth, fixed as much by its own co-ordinates on the map as by the rootless timber of the cross planted in the ground.

Is that really the place where Art's journey ended, or is it just a location that suits the story? It is supported by local tradition from Granabeg just north of the King's River, connecting the fugitives with the striking corrie at the head of Glenreemore, visible to the southeast a couple of miles away and reputedly known as 'Art's Grave'. The first cross was erected in 1932, the year of the Eucharistic Congress and the fifteen-hundredth anniversary of St Patrick's arrival in

Ireland. It was a good year for crosses.

Of course, this tradition might have arisen not from historical fact at all, but from a loose interpretation of what Philip O'Sullivan wrote, or – in the case of Edward Eustace as guide – what he *didn't* write about a western route.

When J. B. Malone, expert on Wicklow landscape and tradition, came to comment on the journey (*Walking in Wicklow*, 1964), he accepted the assumption of Glenreemore as the approach to Glenmalure. He pointed out the junction of two mountain streams on this final stage of the route where a slightly different choice would have reached the destination quickly and easily, and he went on to remark: '… here was made the error that killed Art O'Neill, that crippled Red Hugh O'Donnell for twelve months, and led at length to the Flight of the Earls.' It is an apocalyptic conclusion to say the least, implying that the junction of the Asbawn and Glenree streams, an innocent V on a mountainside, actually points to the collapse of Gaelic Ireland.

Ten miles and many mountains away, an alternative tradition existed at the southeast end of Glenmalure. Local people strongly believed that the fugitives had come that way – heading for the area where the hotel stands today, at Drumgoff crossroads. Research in the 1950s found that the people in one valley had not heard of the tradition in the other. It was also reported that the folklore around Drumgoff was far stronger than that in Granabeg.

For what it's worth, the Drumgoff tradition points to the fugitives having taken the same route as that pursued on the first escape – to the east, towards Glendalough. High above the Glenmalure Hotel, beside an ancient track that long predates the Military Road, there is a battered cairn reputed to be the burial place of Art O'Neill. It is called the Clorawn, from *clocharán*: a heap of stones. Funerals passing by on the way to Glendalough would add a stone to the cairn. The tradition of Art's grave was fully established there. It included the necessary small niche under a crag where the fugitives sheltered, although no one has raised a wooden cross, or even a plaque to rival Glenreemore.

Either route is possible. The O'Byrnes had access to the neighbouring valleys of Glendalough and the Glen of Imaal. There was a rear entry to Glenmalure via the high plateau of Table Mountain at the northwest end. They had mountain access and escape to and from the Pale, the lowlands of Leinster controlled by the English. They were experts in guerrilla defence measures, and the slopes of the narrow valley are thought to have been covered in dense woods with heavy undergrowth.

However, the idea of Fiach MacHugh O'Byrne living in Glenmalure creates a misleading impression today when one can drive to the Baravore Ford at the very end of the narrow, steep valley, almost as far as the *An Óige* Hostel (formerly the house of a gamekeeper). Fiach MacHugh lived at the other, lowland end of the valley, a further six miles or so from the well-known ford at the very back of the Glen. Anyone entering Glenmalure via the upland route associated with Red Hugh had a wearisome distance still to go along the rocky valley to reach sanctuary. Fiach MacHugh O'Byrne's fortified home was at Ballinacor, in the vicinity of Greenane today. The famous guerrilla chieftain lived in a rath-type settlement, with wooden dwellings inside an earthen enclosure, densely hedged for additional protection. This was in direct continuity with the ringfort style of dwelling associated mainly with the early Christian period, around AD 500.

These were largely obsolete by the end of the sixteenth century, but the O'Byrnes were nothing if not traditional. The fact that they had not built a stone tower-house by then testifies to the natural defences of Glenmalure itself.

 FROSTBITE

Red Hugh was carried down to Glenmalure from the grave of Art O'Neill. Except for his feet of clay, he had been brought back to life with the force of a slow resurrection. He was kept in a house hidden in the depths of the woods, where he had care and medical attention. They may have attempted to thaw out his feet with direct heat, placing him close to a fire. That would seem urgent and natural, but it actually worsens the condition. Mountaineers have massaged the frostbitten limbs of their companions, hour after hour, and even flogged the feet with frayed rope-ends, trying to restore circulation. Sadly, it has been revealed that such efforts actually add to the damage, if the cells within the tissue are frozen. Deep frostbite must be left as it is until it can be treated medically.

Frostbitten skin is hard and waxy, like ivory to the touch, until the frost-blisters set in. The flesh of both of Red Hugh's feet was torn and shredded and could not have been massaged by hand, which people do in desperation, instead of warming the frozen limb in a rescuer's groin or armpit. Instead of direct heat, his attendants may have immersed the feet in warm water (a good idea, at about 40°C). Nothing is felt at first, but as the less afflicted areas thaw out, feeling returns to burn like raw electricity.

O'Sullivan claims that Red Hugh had lost his big toenails during the walk, but this classic symptom is more likely to

have occurred later. Anyone with experience of the condition (and perhaps the attendants had, given the harsh winters of the time) would have watched anxiously for the
shadow of gangrene setting in, the putrefaction of ruined
flesh. It is the kiss of ice, as if the toes had kicked through
the shell of survival into the frozen void outside.

Too soon – within a week or two – a messenger came from
Hugh O'Neill, Red Hugh's brother-in-law, no doubt inform-
ing him of political imperatives at home. The messenger, a
close associate of O'Neill's, was the dashingly named Turley
Boy O'Hagan. ('Boy' from *buí:* yellow-haired.) O'Donnell set
off on the tortuous journey northwards. According to information recorded later by the Castle authorities, he bought
two horses at Ballinacor for the journey north, one of them a
'white bobtayl mare'. His feet had not healed and he had to
be helped on and off his horse by O'Hagan. Obviously the
toes were infected by then. The toenails would have black-
ened and lifted off as the shadow deepened.

O'Hagan, who spoke confident English and was familiar
with the authorities, accompanied him all the way. The
route was heavily guarded, and they chose a series of daring
options. Fiach MacHugh O'Byrne sent a troop of Wicklow
horsemen to protect them as far as the River Liffey. They
forded it dangerously close to Dublin, at a deep but un-
guarded spot. Among the horsemen who had come to escort
O'Donnell to the Liffey was one Phelim O'Toole.

Red Hugh and Turley Boy travelled by Drogheda,
Dundalk and Armagh to Dungannon and Ballyshannon. The
journey must have been excruciating for O'Donnell. Injured
feet in motion are particularly vulnerable. They catch on
every obstruction. His biographer strains for a biblical

parallel to celebrate the homecoming, and settles on Moses delivering his people from bondage. However, it was nothing of the kind. Though celebrated as a hero, Red Hugh became an unstable element in Hugh O'Neill's campaign to prise Ireland out from under English rule and into his own control.

As if he had been wound up tight and then set loose, O'Donnell was to make a dizzying set of journeys in the remaining decade of his life, including the night crossing of the frozen bogs of Slievefelim on his way to disaster at Kinsale in 1601. All those journeys were on horseback. Shortly after reaching home from Glenmalure in 1592, he was confined to bed from February to April, and his two big toes were amputated. This was to stop the infection spreading through his body, and it is still the only option in the case of serious, untreated frostbite. In O'Donnell's case, the only question is whether the damage was quite so severe and whether amputation might have been avoided if the wounds had been kept clean. Proper recovery was expected to take a year. After three months, he defied his physicians' orders and called for an assembly of tribal chiefs. His father abdicated at the instigation of Iníon Dubh, and Red Hugh became the 'O'Donnell', chieftain of a dangerously divided people.

He was scarcely out of his twenties when he died in 1602, going out in a hectic blaze of failure. There is no glory in the final winter march from Sligo to the débâcle of Kinsale or in the headlong skite to the Continent that followed. Dramatic to the bitter end, he died mysteriously in Spain. James Blake, known spy and double agent, was on his heels with the declared intention of killing him. Although it seems more likely now that O'Donnell died of natural causes, a bitter whiff of poison haunts his demise. If popular suspicion were a forensic test, Blake would have been hanged ten thousand times.

II

SURVIVAL MARCH

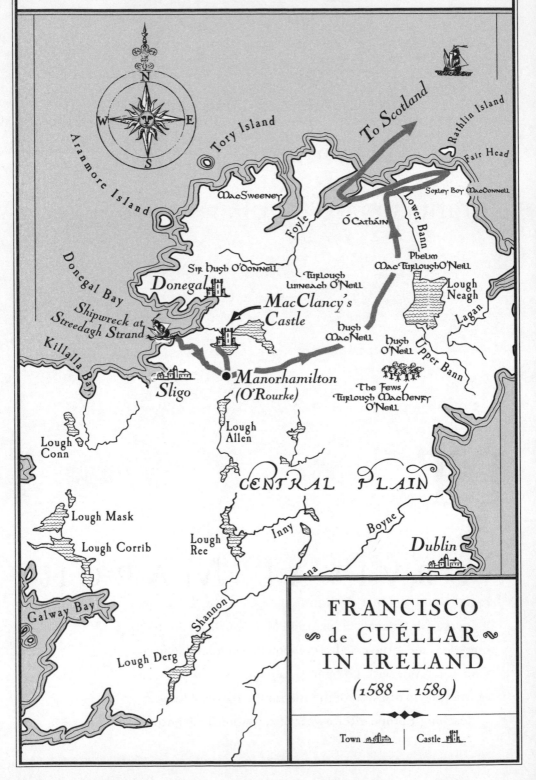

IRELAND

FRANCISCO
de CUÉLLAR
IN IRELAND
(1588 – 1589)

Town | Castle

2 NAKED AMONG THE SAVAGES

The Adventures of Captain Francisco de Cuéllar

(1588–9)

 hipwrecked off the west coast of Ireland in September 1588, Spanish sea-captain Francisco de Cuéllar spent more than seven months attempting to escape with his life from a deeply disordered country on the brink of war. Irish chieftains, O'Rourke, MacClancy, O'Neill and McDonnell, whose territories de Cuéllar traversed, were soon to be embroiled in the Nine Years' War with England, a campaign that would start well and end in disaster for the Irish at the Battle of Kinsale.

Reaching Europe after a year of sensational adventures,

de Cuéllar wrote a detailed account of his Irish travels. Composed in Antwerp, October 1589, his letter, to an unidentified patron in Spain, lay for three centuries in an archive in Madrid. It provides dramatic insights into Irish culture and the tensions dividing it at the time.

> I escaped from the sea ... with over three hundred soldiers who also succeeded in staying alive and swimming ashore. With them I shared extreme misfortunes: naked, barefoot the whole of last winter, more than seven months through mountains and woods, among savages, which all of them are in those parts of Ireland where we ran aground.
>
> FRANCISCO DE CUÉLLAR

 # ATLANTIC STORMS

Early summer, 1588, a fleet of one hundred and thirty ships sailed north from the port of Lisbon, bound for war with England. The Spanish Armada carried eight thousand sailors and twenty thousand soldiers.

Three and a half months later, the Armada was on the run, routed by the English fleet. Trapped in the Straits of Dover, the Spaniards chose the long way home. Rather than fight their way back through the English Channel, they fled up the east coast of England and Scotland. Turning the northern tip of the British Isles in freezing fog, they struggled south along the Atlantic coast of Ireland where storms had been raging for days.

Some vessels crawled into harbours along the coast, desperate for shelter and fresh water. In Galway, an entire crew was executed, in response to the orders of the English lord deputy, Sir William Fitzwilliam. Many vessels were unfit for the heavy seas crashing against them, and they leaked severely. The leverage of mainmasts under sail in heavy weather opened up the planks of others. In all, twenty-six ships were lost and over five thousand men of the Spanish Armada were shipwrecked in the storms that raged along the Irish coast.

SHIPWRECK AT STREEDAGH STRAND

On 21 September, three ships staggered towards Streedagh Strand in Co. Sligo. They were the *Juliana*, *Lavia* and *Santa Maria de Visón*. Failing to round Erris Head, they had hung on their anchor cables for four days off the Sligo coast, until disaster struck, hurling them towards the shore where they struck a reef. They were to lose a thousand men between them, while three hundred at most reached the shore alive.

On the poop of the battered *Lavia*, Francisco de Cuéllar weighed up the disintegrating timbers against the fate awaiting him on the Sligo shore. Men were drowning all around – many inside the actual ships. Others were sluiced into the boiling sea by enormous breakers. Wealthy officers plunged overboard, their clothing laden with coins. They sank immediately between the waves. Certain noblemen had themselves sealed up in a small boat and launched as if it were a barrel. Scores of men clung to it as it entered the water. By the time it reached the strand, it had become a sealed coffin.

The reception awaiting survivors was plainly visible. Hordes of plunderers danced with delight on the beach as the ships broke asunder and booty was washed ashore. Castaways were stripped, beaten and robbed by the Irish *salbajes* – savages. Soldiers of the local garrison robbed the Spaniards and then executed them. 'It did not seem to me,' de Cuéllar remarked later with a rather cool sense of the odds, 'that anything good was happening on any side.'

With only minutes to spare before the hull collapsed, de Cuéllar rescued the Judge Advocate of the Armada, Martín de Aranda, a patron to whom he owed a great debt. They took to a mass of floating wreckage, but it was chained to the *Lavia* and battered by storm-tossed timbers. The unfortunate judge was weighed down with money sewn into his waistcoat and leggings. De Cuéllar managed to seize a floating hatchway about the size of a table. Launching his weight on one end, he overbalanced and sank in deep water, only to come up again and struggle onto the raft. He dragged his patron after him, but a huge wave washed the Judge Advocate away. 'He kept shouting as he was drowning, calling on God.'

As soon as the judge was washed off de Cuéllar's raft, it began to heel over again. At the same moment, a piece of timber smashed down on his legs, dealing him a severe injury, which was to cripple him for months. A sequence of four waves (the detail is precise) washed him onto the shore on Streedagh Strand north of Sligo Bay. This beach, along with others nearby, is a surfer's paradise today, with huge storm-waves rolling in, exactly as de Cuéllar described. He could not swim, but swimming in such conditions was hardly relevant. Bodies were being hurled ashore, dead or alive. The danger on reaching the beach was that a following wave would sweep him back to sea again. Weltering in blood, severely injured, he was an appalling spectacle. The

❧ Sentenced to Death

In his account of the shipwreck, de Cuéllar was careful to underline that he was among the last to abandon the *Lavia*, even though he was not in command. 'Most of the men and all the captains and officers had already drowned and were dead when I resolved to find a way of saving my own life ....'

De Cuéllar had a personal case to make and he made it urgently in his letter. Weeks earlier, in the English Channel, he had been stripped of his command of a galleon called the *San Pedro* and sentenced to a brutal death for lack of attention to duty. Twenty captains in all were sentenced. De Cuéllar's ship, by his own account, had done no worse than to move out of formation in the hands of a bad pilot, while he himself slept from exhaustion. The Judge Advocate, Martín de Aranda, had appealed the cruel conviction to the commander-in-chief, and de Cuéllar's life was spared. Otherwise he would have been hanged from the yardarm. He had remained on board the judge's ship for the journey home. One captain was actually hanged. Returning home in disgrace, his professional honour in shreds, de Cuéllar faced a battle for the recovery of his good name in Spain. The judge who had reprieved him would have been a crucial witness.

Records recently discovered show that his conviction on the Armada was not his first brush with authority. He had already been the subject of an enquiry concerning an incident in Brazil, in 1583, when the Spanish had lost a vessel in a skirmish with the English because de Cuéllar had kept his own ship out of the firing line. It should be remembered that few of the Armada captains were experienced commanders and that very heavy-handed discipline prevailed.

plunderers stripping other survivors somehow left him alone. He made a distinction between 'enemies and savages' on the beach: the enemy English and the native Irish. He missed the point that the soldiers killing his own countrymen were largely Irish too.

Not only were the clothes of the castaways of value to the plunderers, dressed themselves in woollen homespun, but they knew that the Spaniards carried their valuables either on their bodies, or stitched into their clothing, as de Cuéllar was soon to reveal. He seems to have crawled away from the beach, without drawing attention to himself, until at nightfall he lay down 'on some rushes, in open country and in great pain.' He had seen other Spaniards in extreme misery on the way.

The *salbajes* did not necessarily kill their victims as the soldiers did, but they beat them into a condition in which they could be stripped, robbed and cast aside. Added to hypothermia and the horror of shipwreck, this brutality left many stark naked, 'with not a single garment on them', and must have induced a condition of extreme shock. The symptoms, so familiar today in casualties, are obvious in de Cuéllar's encounter with a young Spaniard who was naked and so shocked that he could not speak. De Cuéllar himself was still dressed in a blood-drenched shirt and some kind of jacket. Lying on open ground, the Spaniards were discovered by two menacing Irishmen who arrived after dark. One had a gun and the other carried an axe. In one of the many ironies in de Cuéllar's account, the strangers took pity on the Spanish pair. Cutting a mass of rushes, they covered them well. 'Then they went to the strand to ransack and break open chests and whatever they found there.' During the night, de Cuéllar heard further pillagers arriving on horseback. By then, his young companion had perished from exposure. His death greatly upset de Cuéllar, as did the fate of all the other bodies 'that the sea had cast up, to be devoured by ravens and wolves, with no one to give any of them burial ....'

The Abbey of Staad

At daybreak, he began to search for a nearby church. This was the Abbey of Staad (*Stad* – a stopping place), a few hundred metres from the southern end of Streedagh, although not visible from the beach itself. The gable of the tiny abbey still stands, just above the shoreline, looking out to the monastic island of Inishmurray, which it served as a departure point and a mainland sanctuary. The once-sturdy gable is now a tissue of loose masonry, showing clearly the use of seashells for lime in the mortar between the fine blocks of local stone.

When de Cuéllar reached it, the church was abandoned, its contents burned and destroyed. '… all the friars had fled to the hills for fear of the enemies who would sacrifice them too if they caught them.' A grisly scene confronted him within. Twelve of his countrymen had been executed and their naked bodies were left hanging from iron bars. De Cuéllar must have suspected that his own nagging appointment with the hangman might not be postponed indefinitely. He had escaped the noose on the Armada, only to find it waiting for him ashore.

Escaping through a nearby wood, he met an old woman who was hiding five or six cows from soldiers billeted in her village. They were there, presumably, to deal with the Spanish castaways, and were more than likely Irish themselves. Throughout the country, most of the soldiers in the English army were actually Irishmen. These were probably from Sir Richard Bingham's garrison in Sligo town.

With tears and sign language, the old woman warned de Cuéllar not to approach the village as the enemy had already chopped the heads off many Spanish there. Injured and starving, he made his way back towards the beach where parties were still scavenging among the wreckage and carrying away the loot. There must have been an untold wealth of ropes and rigging, timber and exotic effects, coming ashore. The local people would have been competing for the salvage with the garrisons and with Elizabethan officials.

✤ The Spanish Ships

A map of Sligo, drawn in early 1589, shows a colossal mainmast, rigged and flagged, lying along miles of coastline. A caption says: 'The wrack of trý Spanesh Shepps'. The crude drawing echoes the opinion of an English observer who reported a mast as big as any two he had ever seen before. These were enormous ships. Divers on the wreck of the *Juliana* in 1985 discovered the rudder, intact, with its iron swivels still in position. The rudder is twelve metres long.

Terrified of capture, de Cuéllar remained in hiding nearby, where he was joined by two Spanish soldiers. They were naked, one with a head wound sustained while being robbed. According to them, the English had already executed more than a hundred Spaniards. Since things could get no worse and he was dying of starvation anyway, de Cuéllar headed for the wreckage in the hope of salvaging some ship's biscuit from the tide. On the way, he recognised, among hundreds of corpses on the shore, the bodies of comrades and superiors.

With the aid of the two soldiers, he dug a pit in the sand to bury some of the most distinguished victims, including a captain who had been a close friend of his. They were mobbed at once by savages: two hundred and fifty of them, in de Cuéllar's estimation. He explained in sign language that they were burying their friends to protect their bodies from the ravens. The Spaniards were spared, perhaps as a result of these corporal works of mercy, but not for long. De Cuéllar was still clothed and he was soon attacked by four men determined to rob him. He was unexpectedly defended by a chief of some kind, who ordered the assailants away. 'He must have been a chief because they respected him,' de Cuéllar observed. This mentor spent some time with the Spaniards, before pointing them to a track leading to his own village.

THE VILLAGE OF GRANGE

Barefoot on stony ground, tormented by his injury, de Cuéllar became separated from his companions. He excused them wholeheartedly on the grounds that they were naked and freezing and thoroughly justified in going ahead without him. The fine sand of Streedagh must have irritated his open wound. His leg would later become infected. Behind the dunes, a muddy lagoon led to wooded ground. Dragging himself inland, de Cuéllar could not have guessed that he was beginning a journey of seven months, during which he would wander throughout northern Ireland under constant threat of discovery and death. His first tottering steps took him upriver towards a settlement of thatched huts where the village of Grange now stands.

It seems likely that Grange was not a secular village at the time, but an out-farm belonging to the Cistercian Abbey thirty-five miles away in Boyle, Co. Roscommon. This outfarm, with its buildings and over five hundred acres of land, would have been occupied by monks and farm-workers, although they may well have gone into hiding during the military disturbance.

As he made his painful way towards the 'village', de Cuéllar would have found his view dominated by the unique rampart of Benbulben's northwest face, about three miles away. The mountain at this point appears as an enormous, green *mesa*, deeply fluted with symmetrical gullies. De Cuéllar never mentions this extraordinary landmark, and it is possible that the clouds were clamped down low enough to obscure it.

He measured his crippled progress in arquebus-shots, *tyros de arcabuz*, just as another might use the flight of an arrow. The arquebus was a contemporary firearm, lighter than a musket, with a limited range of perhaps a couple of hundred metres. He had covered two such measures when he was assaulted again. This strange encounter, too odd to be a fabrication, shows the kind of mixture that could be thrown together in a peasant society in a time of upheaval. The group he met consisted of an elderly *salbaje*, his twenty-year-old daughter, and two armed soldiers – one English, the other French. The young woman was *hermossísima por todo estremo*, beautiful in the extreme. She was also, in de Cuéllar's opinion, mistress to the English soldier.

The group was on its way to plunder the Spanish ships, along with the rest of the population. De Cuéllar was attacked by the English soldier who succeeded in slashing him before the others separated them. The old peasant, remembering his obligations as a savage, stepped in and robbed de Cuéllar, stripping him of his clothes. Under the linen shirt, he wore a valuable gold chain, and in his jerkin – a kind of waistcoat – he carried forty-five gold *escudos*, two months' worth of a captain's salary.

The girl, upset by the mistreatment rather than the theft, intervened, and he got his doublet back, though not the linen shirt, and certainly not the money or the chain. He seems at this point to have had some kind of outer jacket *(sayo)* as well as the waistcoat. The girl coveted the holy relics he wore around his neck in a scapular. She took them for herself, claiming that she was a Christian, which, in de Cuéllar's sardonic opinion, 'she was – as much as Mohammed'. He was left on his own then, bleeding badly from the new wound, while the group returned to their hut. But the image of Irish hospitality was restored by a boy sent out with a poultice for the injury and a meal of 'butter, milk and a piece of oaten bread'. The boy led him along the road, avoiding the soldiers at Grange. He owed this service to the kindness of the French soldier rather than to the old savage or his daughter.

De Cuéllar's description of his actual route is vague, although events are immediate and striking. The boy pointed out to him mountains in the distance, behind which an important savage chieftain, *un gran senor salbaje,* lived. This chieftain, Brian O'Rourke of Breifne, was already on the verge of rebellion. He was taking in all the naked Spaniards who reached him, and more than eighty survivors had already arrived in Co. Leitrim. O'Rourke's lands lay to the east of Benbulben and the limestone plateau known as the Dartry Mountains.

❊ Into Leitrim

De Cuéllar's journey in search of protection could have taken any one of a number of routes, depending on which of O'Rourke's settlements – Manorhamilton or Dromahair – he was to reach. Earlier commentators favour a plausible route via Glenade to Glencar, but Cruickshank and Gallagher in 1988 suggest a very different route, just north of Lough Gill to Dromahair. Either way, the journey is roughly twenty miles (thirty kilometres). De Cuéllar was regaining strength and beginning to cover greater distances, although still injured and virtually starving. Without diminishing his achievement, it might be noted that he was travelling in the season of wild berries, fruit and corn. Hazel nuts, though not ripe yet, should have been plentiful in a limestone landscape.

His opinion of the Irish improved when he was taken in for the night by some noble natives. One of them spoke Latin – not particularly unusual in sixteenth-century Ireland. He dressed de Cuéllar's wounds, fed him and gave him a bed. Later that night, the man's father and brothers came in, laden with material from the wreckage. They too made de Cuéllar welcome. Given their behaviour, it has been suggested that these men might have been monks in hiding, perhaps from the Cistercian grange itself, the father being the abbot and the others monks.

In the morning, they dispatched a boy and a horse to take de Cuéllar along a section of the route where the mud was belly-deep – perhaps a detour through a bog. The boy spotted a troop of horsemen riding towards them at speed, and he hid de Cuéllar behind some rocks. Over a hundred and fifty horsemen passed, 'on their way to the strand to rob and kill any Spaniards they found'. De Cuéllar, in this instance, used the Gaelic term, *Sasanach*, for an Englishman, which he rendered in Spanish as *sásanas*. He may also have adopted the Irish practice (evident in the annals) of exaggerating the enemy numbers.

Having escaped detection, and still on horseback with his guide, de Cuéllar fell immediately into the hands of 'more than forty savages on foot' who wanted to cut him to pieces, 'because they were all Lutherans'.

The boy persuaded them that the Spaniard was already a captive of his master, and they contented themselves with beating him and stealing every stitch of clothing he wore, so that he was left naked as the day he was born. At this point, de Cuéllar admits, he lost the will to survive and he prayed for death. But he rallied as usual, and continued on his way.

 # GLENADE LOUGH

Sheltering that night in a deserted hut by a lake (long assumed to have been Glenade Lough), he found three men, 'naked as the day they were born', hiding in the hut among sheaves of straw. De Cuéllar was attired by then in ferns and a bit of straw matting, and both parties prayed aloud in frightened Spanish on sight of each other. The three had just lost eight companions to a murderous mob. When they discovered that he was not only human but that he was actually Captain de Cuéllar, they were overjoyed and, as he says proudly, 'they rushed up to me and nearly finished me off completely, embracing me.' The group slept there that night, having eaten nothing but blackberries and watercress.

All the following day, until nightfall, they were trapped in

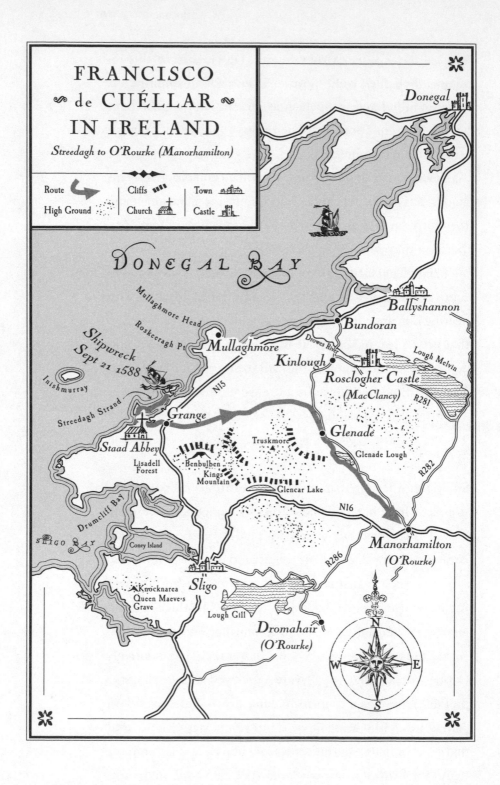

DONEGAL BAY

Donegal

Ballyshannon

Bundoran

Mullaghmore Head

Roskeeragh Pt

Mullaghmore

Drowes River

Kinlough

Lough Melvin

Shipwreck
Sept 21 1588

Inishmurray

Rosclogher Castle
(MacClancy)

R281

N15

Streedagh Strand

Grange

Staad Abbey

Lisadell
Forest

Benbulben
Kings
Mountain

Truskmore

Glenade

Glenade Lough

R282

Drumcliff Bay

Glencar Lake

N16

SLIGO BAY

Coney Island

Manorhamilton
(O'Rourke)

Knocknarea
Queen Maeve's
Grave

Sligo

R286

Lough Gill

Dromahair
(O'Rourke)

N
W   E
S

the hut by a party of savages working outside, whom the Spaniards judged to be hostile. Eventually, resuming their journey before dawn on the second day, they found themselves in friendlier country, with 'huts inhabited by better people who, though all savages, were Christians and charitable.' One man took de Cuéllar into his family hut and patched him up, refusing to let him leave until he had recovered sufficiently to reach O'Rourke's village – whether Manorhamilton or Dromahair. Oddly enough, these charitable Christians did not give their guest a bit of clothing, such as a cloak which would have disguised him as Irish, because he reached the village still wrapped in a piece of matting.

Unfortunately, *el senor de Ruerge* was not at home. He was away defending threatened territory, and some seventy refugees, all in desperate straits, awaited his return. They were not effusively welcomed in O'Rourke's absence, although de Cuéllar's condition aroused great pity in all who saw him, according to his own account, which openly uses such devices to give the reader a sense of his condition, heightened by bursts of piety and a healthy sense of humour.

 ## LOST IN DONEGAL

While begging for scraps of food next morning, he heard that a big ship had arrived on the coast further north, to pick up survivors. With a score of Spaniards, he set off immediately. Again, because of his injuries, he fell behind on the journey to the port, which was either Killybegs or Donegal itself. The Armada ship had put in for repairs after the gales. Setting sail before de Cuéllar reached the port, the overloaded ship was wrecked further along the coast, with all of his recent

❧ Captain de Leyva and the Girona

On 21 September, the day of the Streedagh disaster, the *Rata Encoronada*, under the extraordinary Captain de Leyva, had run aground at Ballycroy, Co. Mayo. De Leyva, who was provisional commander-in-chief of the Armada, burnt the wreck to deprive the enemy of plunder, took his men safely ashore, and occupied a nearby castle. According to contemporary accounts, he marched to another ship farther along the Mayo coast. He took command and set sail for Scotland with two crews on board. Wrecked again off the coast of Donegal, in Loughros More Bay, he occupied an island-fort in Kiltoorish lake (where one of his heavy guns remained until it was stolen in the 1970s.) From Ardara, he marched his men twenty miles south across the steep peninsula to join the fateful *Girona* at Killybegs. She was, of course, wrecked off Co. Antrim and only nine of the thirteen hundred men de Leyva had marshalled from various wrecks escaped to Scotland. The movements of this large body of armed men and their potential alliances with rebel chieftains, such as Onelli (O'Neill) and Horruerk (O'Rourke), were reported to both the Spanish and the English authorities.

companions on board. All hands were lost. We do not know which of the Armada ships this was.

De Cuéllar had been spared a second shipwreck (if not more), but now he was alone again and lost somewhere in south Donegal. Strangely, the O'Donnells – chieftains of the region, with their main castle in Donegal town – are not mentioned. De Cuéllar might easily have gone to them. He could not have known it, but they were to deal less than honourably with a number of Spaniards who came into their control. They attempted to trade them with the authorities in Dublin for the release of Red Hugh O'Donnell. The Spaniards were accepted by the English and promptly executed in Dublin Castle. Red Hugh was not released.

MacClancy's Castle

On the road, de Cuéllar met a priest in lay clothing, who spoke with him in Latin. The priest fed him and directed him to the castle of another chieftain, a day's march away to the southeast. This was the home of Tadhg MacClancy, a chief subject to O'Rourke. MacClancy's castle at Rosclogher was built on a fortified *crannóg*, or artificial island, about a hundred metres off the south shore of Lough Melvin. The castle, ruined now though the *crannóg* and foundations are still dramatically visible, is close to the present-day village of Kinlough.

 # To Hell and Back

Before he could reach this sanctuary, de Cuéllar was kidnapped by a blacksmith living in some isolated place with an old witch he kept for a wife, *una maldita bieja que tenía por muger*. In fear of his life, the Spaniard was forced to work the bellows for more than a week, smiling pleasantly all the while to appease his captors. In a sense, this reads like a symbolic dream of purgatory or of hell, brought to a halt when the disguised priest arrived on the scene by chance and sent some of MacClancy's men to rescue him. When de Cuéllar reached the chieftain's settlement at Rosclogher, on the lakeshore, he was still dressed in straw. There were eight or ten Spaniards already there. Indeed, one had already assisted in his liberation from the forge. A note of quivering pathos is struck on his arrival at MacClancy's castle: 'His women even wept to see how badly I had been treated.'

De Cuéllar's troubles seemed over at last. Dressed in an Irish cloak, he became very friendly with the ladies,

❧ *The Irish*

De Cuéllar switched his attention from his own adventures to describe the local Irish in a famous passage that defies compression:

They live in thatched cabins and are all big men, handsome and well-built, and swift as the red deer. They eat only once a day, and this has to be at night, and what they normally eat is butter and oaten bread. They drink buttermilk, for they have no other drink. And they don't drink water, though it's the best in the world. On feast-days they eat some kind of half-cooked meat, with neither bread nor salt, for that is their custom. They dress accordingly, in tight hose and short loose coats of very coarse goat's hair. They wrap up in blankets and wear their hair down to their eyes. They are great travellers and they are inured to hardship; they are continually at war with the English garrisoned there by the Queen. Against these they defend themselves and don't let them into their lands, which are all flooded and marshy: the whole area is more than forty leagues long and wide.

What these people are most inclined to is thieving and robbing one another; so that not a day passes among them without a call-to-arms, because as soon as the people in the next village find out that in this one there are cattle or anything else, they come armed at night and all hell breaks loose and they slaughter one another. And as soon as the English from the garrisons find out who has rounded up and stolen the most cattle, they are sent in to seize them. All that these people can do is to retreat into the mountains with their women and herds, for they have no other property, furniture or clothes. They sleep on the floor, on freshly-cut rushes, full of water and ice. Most of the women are very beautiful, but badly turned out: they wear no more than a shift, and a shawl that they wrap round themselves, and a piece of linen on their heads which is folded several times and knotted at the forehead. They work hard, and are good housekeepers, in their own way ....

TRANS: GALLAGHER & CRUICKSHANK, *GOD'S OBVIOUS DESIGN*

including MacClancy's wife, and they treated him well. He was to spend three months with them, becoming as savage as themselves, *hecho propio salbaje como ellos,* in a nice variation on the cliché of the stranger who becomes more Irish than the Irish themselves. Obviously a cheerful fellow, he developed a reputation as a fortune teller and palm-reader, 'telling them a great deal of nonsense'. He was in great demand, and he reflected that his troubles must be over since he could hardly fall much lower than to be a gypsy among savages. He became so popular among the women that MacClancy himself had to give orders that his guest was not to be pestered any further.

FITZWILLIAM MARCHES WEST

Meanwhile, Sir William Fitzwilliam, Lord Deputy of Ireland, was marching hastily westwards from Dublin, to suppress whatever threat the Spaniards might pose. On his orders, survivors were being exterminated, except for those isolated groups protected by MacClancy, O'Rourke, O'Neill, Sorley Boy MacDonnell, and a few other chieftains. And, of course, the fifteen hundred men de Leyva had assembled in Donegal, two hundred of whom had to be left behind by the *Girona,* while the rest sailed to their doom.

As the English army drew close to Rosclogher Castle, leaving a trail of destruction in its wake, MacClancy decided to withdraw for safety into the hills with his people and his cattle. He was in a towering rage, his hair down round his eyes in the Irish fringe, the *glib.* De Cuéllar advised him to calm down a bit while the Spaniards consulted among themselves. The former ship's captain gave his countrymen a gallant speech. They should make a stand, he said, and refuse to run any further. He argued that they should occupy the castle by themselves – all nine of them – and defend it against the English army, which he believed to number about seventeen hundred men. His strategy was based on the impregnability of MacClancy's island castle and on the difficulty of the terrain surrounding the lake. Neither claim was strictly true, and artillery would have toppled his case overnight.

Siege at MacClancy's Castle

MacClancy stocked the castle with small arms and supplies, including several boatloads of stones. There is no mention among the weapons of a *pedrero,* a gun to fire the stones, so they might have been meant for throwing if things got really bad. Finally, de Cuéllar swore an oath to MacClancy that he would not abandon Rosclogher, or hand it over to the enemy under any circumstances, even if he were dying of hunger. In exacting this oath, MacClancy seems to have anticipated the kind of betrayals that would occur in Munster a dozen years later, after the Battle of Kinsale, when certain Spanish commanders were quick to negotiate with the enemy.

Engagingly brash, de Cuéllar boasts that their courage was admired all over the territory. Not by the English, however. When Fitzwilliam's forces drew up at Rosfriar point, a kilometre away from the castle, they hanged two Spaniards on the lakeshore. The noose was winking at de Cuéllar again.

In the face of threats and offers, he refused to yield. His men went so far as to give cheek to the English from the castle walls, claiming that they could not hear the threats.

Fitzwilliam's men besieged Rosclogher for seventeen days, until winter closed in with gales and blizzards and sent the army packing, all the way back to Dublin. MacClancy returned and greeted the Spaniards as heroes. He offered his sister in marriage to de Cuéllar, who declined. He gives no opinion as to her appearance, which is not a good sign. Earlier, he had remarked that MacClancy's own wife was extremely beautiful and he may have been unwilling to accept less. But all he asked, according to himself, was a guide to take him to a place where he might find a boat going north. (King James of Scotland was friendly to Spain.) His request was not granted and he realised that he was a prisoner rather than a guest. MacClancy meant to keep the Spaniards as a line of defence. In fact, this policy was widespread among

∾ The Fate of MacClancy and O'Rourke

What de Cuéllar in his boyish pride could not know was that within a couple of years, both of the savage chieftains he admired for their hostility to the Lutheran Queen – Brian O'Rourke and Tadhg MacClancy – would be dead in brutal circumstances. MacClancy, trapped by the soldiers of the murderous Sir George Bingham, plunged into the lake and tried to swim to Rosclogher Castle. A shot broke his arm. Dragged ashore, he was killed and beheaded. A comment in State Papers of 23 April 1590, concludes: 'He was the most barbarous creature in Ireland ....' The remark could have been applied more aptly to George Bingham himself, or to his brother Richard, provincial president of Connacht. In the same year, Brian O'Rourke of Breifne fled to Scotland. He was arrested and brought to London where he was hanged.

Irish chieftains in the north, several of whom saw the Spaniards as a kind of military currency for settling local scores among themselves – a role the castaways were unwilling to perform. A couple of hours before dawn, on 4 January 1589, de Cuéllar and four others quit the castle on Lough Melvin and took to the road again.

Across Ulster to North Antrim

De Cuéllar travelled for twenty days, traversing Ulster in January to reach the north of Co. Antrim. Known as 'the Route', this was the territory of Sorley Boy MacDonnell, a chieftain of Scottish extraction who maintained an ambiguous relationship with the English authorities. Sorley Boy (*buí*: yellow or fair-haired) had already salvaged guns from the wrecked *Girona* and had helped Spanish survivors to reach Scotland.

De Cuéllar's journey cross-country had taken him 'through mountains and deserted places, with great hardship', meaning that he avoided contact with people as much as possible, for fear of capture or betrayal. In the middle of winter, in one of the worst periods of weather in recent Irish history, food must have been very difficult to come by. The journey took him through the lands of the various O'Neills, and past the territory of Ó Catháin, *el Ocán*, a vassal-chieftain of the O'Neills. On the north Antrim coast, de Cuéllar was devastated by the evidence of the *Girona* shipwreck. This great galleon would have been a symbol of Spanish invincibility and pride. Everywhere he went, people told him harrowing tales and showed him Spanish valuables. Spain must have seemed sadly diminished and very far away. There were no boats at all bound for Scotland, so he limped painfully back along the north Antrim coast to the territory of Ó Catháin (east of Lough Foyle), to discover that he had missed a sailing and that Ó Catháin was having nothing further to do with Spaniards. He had already exerted himself on their behalf and now there were English soldiers everywhere.

His leg-wound, which must have involved a recurrent infection, felled de Cuéllar again in a dangerous military area, but he was rescued by some women who hid him in their cabins on the mountain for six weeks, until the wound had healed. Unfortunately, he tells us nothing about the people who performed such an extraordinary service.

There were beautiful girls in the next episode, however, in the thatched cabins of a village where soldiers were usually billeted. De Cuéllar's Irish must have been improving. While the military were away on an engagement, he became friendly with the girls, visiting them for company and conversation. It is a safe bet that he resorted to palm-reading and fortune telling again. Two soldiers captured him in the house and began to make arrangements for his transport to prison in Dublin. Thinking that he was incapacitated and quite willing to be taken, the soldiers began to romp with the girls, *retocar con las mocas*. Their mother tipped de Cuéllar the wink and he slipped out the door and away.

 # LOUGH FOYLE

He found shelter with a family of rebels on a hill overlooking Lough Foyle. A boy went back to the village after a day or two and found the soldiers still rushing around in a rage, looking for de Cuéllar. He was soon on his way to the home of another potential patron. The man in question is understood to have been Redmond Gallagher, Bishop of Derry, although de Cuéllar leaves his identity vague. 'This bishop was a very good Christian; he went about dressed as a savage so as to pass unnoticed.' But he knew he had reached sanctuary at last and he could not restrain his tears at the encounter. It seems that the bishop was also pleased – especially when he learned that de Cuéllar was a captain, no less. A week later, the Spaniard was on a vessel travelling north. It was 'a miserable little boat with eighteen people on board.'

∾ *Bloodbath at Lough Foyle*

A savage massacre of Spanish castaways had taken place near Lough Foyle after the *Trinidad Valencera* was wrecked in Kinnagoe Bay. Five hundred survivors, marching through the countryside, surrendered to an English force commanded by Major Kelly, obviously an Irishman. The Spanish officers were separated out, to be held for ransom, while their unarmed men were shot down in cold blood in front of their horrified eyes. According to witnesses, three hundred Spaniards were killed on the orders of Major Kelly and the notorious Hovenden brothers, two captains distinguished in Spanish reports by their long, white beards.

Conor O'Devany, Bishop of Down and Connor, took in one hundred and fifty survivors of this massacre. The wounded were taken by Ó Catháin who cared for them until he managed to transfer them to Sorley Boy MacDonnell, chieftain of north Antrim, who succeeded finally in shipping them to Scotland.

# Bound for Scotland

The weather promptly turned bad, a reminder yet again that while de Cuéllar was fortunate in the broad sense of survival, he was very unlucky in the detail. The boat was hurled as far as the Hebrides, although de Cuéllar thought they were the Shetlands. Interestingly, he had also thought that the Mayo coast was Cape Clear in Co. Cork. It took three leaky, swilling days for the boat to fight its way back around the coast of Scotland to its homeport.

The arrival was euphoric, because King James was known to have welcomed survivors of the Armada to Scotland already. By all reports, he had fed and clothed them and paid for their passage home. Sadly, de Cuéllar found 'the opposite was true, for he didn't look after any of them, and not a penny did he give in alms, though the six hundred of us Spaniards who came to that kingdom suffered the direst privations.' The Spaniards waited six miserable months in Scotland, in constant fear of being handed over to the English by James; *porque el rey de Escocia no es nada...* 'for the king of Scotland is nothing ... and he doesn't take a step or eat a scrap except by order of the Queen.'

According to de Cuéllar, it was the constant intervention of Catholic nobles on their behalf that eventually delivered the Spaniards from the Lutheran heretics in the population. In his opinion, the Scottish Catholics prayed constantly that King Philip of Spain would take over their country, 'to restore God's Church'. Of course, there were Irish too who harboured the same hope for their own country

To Flanders

At last, the Duke of Parma negotiated the repatriation of the refugees from Scotland to Flanders in northern Europe, with safe passage through the North Sea promised by the English. The men were transported on four ships by a Scottish merchant who was paid a rate of five *ducats* per head (when a labourer's wage was two *ducats* a month.) The ships were ambushed near Dunkirk by the Dutch fleet – with the connivance of the English, in de Cuéllar's bitter opinion. Two hundred and seventy Spaniards – in two ships – were captured by the Dutch, while the other two vessels ran aground under heavy fire. Hundreds of men were forced to take to the water on planks. De Cuéllar came ashore in Flanders, almost naked again, and in a wretched state. The Dutch, in full sight of the survivors, slaughtered the two hundred and seventy Spaniards they had captured.

De Cuéllar's letter closed with the information that the Spanish had since turned the tables and had beheaded more than four hundred Dutchmen. On a note of grim satisfaction, he concluded: 'This is what I wanted to write to you about. From the city of Antwerp, 4th October 1589.'

De Cuéllar is widely believed to have survived and returned to Spain, although no definite evidence has yet appeared.

3 THE HUNGRY ROAD

March of O'Sullivan Beare

(1602–3)

fter a surge of success, the rebellion known as the Nine Years' War had collapsed in disaster for the Irish, at the Battle of Kinsale, 1601.

A year later, the country was on the verge of famine; racked by defections, reprisals and dispossession. Hugh O'Neill, leader of the rebels, had retreated to Ulster, where he was reported to be still at war. Red Hugh O'Donnell, seeking further aid, had dashed off to Spain where he died in ugly circumstances. Isolated rebels still held out in their own areas. Among these were O'Rourke in Co. Leitrim and O'Sullivan Beare in west Cork.

IRELAND
N
S
E
W
Tory Island
Fair Head
Lower Bann
Foyle
Lough Neagh
Lagan
Upper Bann
Donegal Bay
Erne
Lough Allen
Achill Island
Leitrim
Carlingford Lough
Ballinlough
Curlew Mts.
Clew Bay
CENTRAL PLAIN
Ballymoe
Lough Ree
Glinsk
Inny
Boyne
Slyne Head
Ballygar
Dublin
Ahascragh
Ballinasloe
Dublin Bay
Brosna
Liffey
Aughrim
Galway Bay
Shannon
MacEgan Castle
Barrow
Lough Derg
Limerick
Hollyford
Slaney
Loop Head
Nore
Silvermines Mts.
Donohill
Solohead
Suir
Ballybahellagh
Ardpatrick
Carnsore Point
Blackwater
Millstreet
Hook Head
Cork
Eachros
Ballyvourney
Lee
Glengarriff
Dunboy Castle
Bandon
Bantry
Kinsale
Beara Peninsula
Mizen Head
ATLANTIC
MARCH OF O'SULLIVAN BEARE
West Cork to Leitrim
(31 December 1602 – 14 January 1603)
Route of O'Sullivan Beare March
Town
Church
Castle

 DONAL CAM

Donal O'Sullivan, chieftain of Beare and Bantry, was reduced to a small force of guerrillas and the herds on which they depended for survival. Groups of mercenaries had abandoned him already in the face of disaster. Under relentless pursuit by the English, he was cornered in the oak woods of Glengarriff. His territory had shrunk to a few rocky hills and boggy valleys, from which he was soon to be dislodged.

Forty years old, O'Sullivan had gained the nickname Donal *Cam*, meaning crooked, possibly from a shoulder injury. In an existing portrait, his head is cradled in the ridiculous ruff of the time. He looks refined, almost effete, with sharp features and a cats-whisker moustache. A man of action, he is shown holding weapons in both hands.

❧ *The Beara Peninsula*

The Beara peninsula, O'Sullivan's stronghold, is the ring finger of the Munster coast, Dursey Island a hangnail at the tip. Beara reaches southwestward into the Atlantic below the plump digit of Iveragh and the pointing index of Dingle. The Miskish and Caha Mountains flex like knuckles along its length, jointed across the Healy Pass.

Glengarriff, at the back of Bantry Bay, marks the entrance to the west-Cork peninsula. The little town, unashamedly a tourist trap, is pinned against the sea by the most intricate landscape in Ireland. Sandstone ridges run riot like fossilised waves. They rear up as mountains and subside again into ribs and reefs breaking through the skin of the bog. Wandering roads wind through creases in the rock to spill into hidden valleys.

On the Ordnance Survey maps, sheets 84–5, the peninsula is pocked and measled with the red dots that mark prehistory: standing stones, megalithic tombs, ringforts, rock-art .... Cosmopolitan today, Beara was always somebody's terrain, a complex homeland of the past.

BANTRY BAY

In late December 1602, two armies camped within a couple of miles of each other in the maze of rock and forest between Bantry Bay and the mountains. One, O'Sullivan's guerrilla force, was hidden in the oak-woods of Derrynafulla (*Doire na fola*: oak-wood of the blood). The other was a substantial English army, mopping up the remnants of Munster rebellion. Sir Charles Wilmot, newly appointed governor of Beara, had squeezed several thousand men into a low-lying, open area, to block the passage between the mountains and the sea. The ground was boggy in all its sumps and hollows. The soldiers had permanently soaking feet and wet blankets. They were prone to a fatal ague, a fever of the Irish campaigns. Wilmot's army was English in function and in name. But the vast majority of the soldiers – more than eighty per cent – were Irish. The same was generally true of Queen Elizabeth's forces throughout the country.

When the final battle broke out, Wilmot made a checkmate move. He captured the O'Sullivan herd: two thousand cattle and four thousand sheep. In a stroke, O'Sullivan was stripped of his means of survival. Without milk, butter or meat, his people were reduced to ruin. Wilmot's Irish knew exactly where the animals were pastured, in the coombs and valleys that are tucked like secret pockets around Derrynafulla. The battle for the herd raged for at least six hours, with O'Sullivan's men, in desperation, giving chase right up to the enemy camp.

Cattle-raiding was a standard strategy of war; it was second nature in a culture where wealth was measured in livestock. The Irish did not make hay, and the herds depended on grazing throughout the year. Food was always scarce in winter as many cows were in calf and consequently dry. Oatmeal, the other staple, was in short supply. The campaign against the rebels had already used starvation tactics. Crops were burned all over Beara. Similar action had brought famine and plague to parts of Munster only twenty years before. With the herd, O'Sullivan also lost one hundred ponies, *gearráin*, the tough horses fundamental to transport in rugged terrain.

The herd, known as *caoruigheacht* or *creacht*, had been amassed partly by the raids O'Sullivan had launched in the surrounding areas throughout the year. No doubt, some of his local enemies were getting their own back. The O'Sullivans themselves were split. One faction of the extended family supported the forces of the Crown. Donal's cousin, Owen, had fought on the English side at Kinsale. The two had been bitter enemies since a legal clash for the chieftaincy had been re-solved in Donal's favour. Throughout Ireland, many major families were similarly split, with an Irish faction and a Crown rump. Strength and survival were a gamble of allegiance. But such divisions made resistance hopeless.

Within days of the battle, O'Sullivan's stand had collapsed. Contingents of hired soldiers had already melted away to the north. Others would soon follow. It was not desertion. These were jobbing soldiers, journeymen fighters, tradesmen of a kind. The stink of a lost cause was like a whiff of gangrene to them. Mercenaries worked for wages, not for ideals.

 # VENGEANCE

The aged, the wounded and the sick remained in the woods of Derrynafulla, while the rest slipped away under cover of darkness. There is a tradition that they stoked the campfires to give the impression that O'Sullivan was still there, licking his wounds, preparing for surrender. It would be four or five days before Wilmot's men discovered the deception. This motif occurs in stories worldwide. It has the ring of myth, but it represents a different kind of truth, a necessary fiction, a victory of spirit in defeat.

What was Wilmot doing during those four days? Perhaps he felt no need to suffer losses in a further attack when he could starve O'Sullivan out. When the woods were finally raided, the derelict remnants were put to death.

This callous dispatch of the wounded has been depicted as brutality, which indeed it was. But, at the time, it was nothing out of the ordinary, either to the Irish or the English. If Wilmot's soldiers, probably Irish anyway, had left the victims to starve, that would have seemed equally cruel. Afterwards, Wilmot's army ravaged and burned Beara, leaving it a wasteland, and that too was a crime against humanity. But that is also what the Irish leader, Red Hugh O'Donnell, had done to the lands of his enemies on his own march south to Kinsale a couple of years before, sowing the bitterness his soldiers would harvest on their harrowing retreat. In a land wasted by war, that same vengeance lay in wait for O'Sullivan.

Abandoning Beara, he began the epic march of survival northwards, which would come to symbolise the tragic instability of its time – a journey through hunger and hostility, into the teeth of winter, through a country where loyalty was being bought, sold and betrayed. His followers numbered just over one thousand, of whom four hundred were fighting-men. Thirteen of these were cavalry, the rest foot soldiers. There were six hundred non-combatants – campfollowers, porters, servants, grooms, dependants of one kind or another. Were they an army? Was it a march, a retreat, or a flight? Depending on the point of view, it was at different times all three. The soldiers were guerrillas; the civilians were fugitives. They would be reduced to refugees, and finally to survivors.

From the beginning, they carried a quantity of gold, sent to O'Sullivan from Spain, instead of the soldiers he needed. It was virtually useless, as nobody had anything to sell. There was also a heavy load of lead for the muskets. There must have been moments when they wished they could dump the lead and fire the Spanish gold instead. The fact that they kept their gunpowder dry, day after day, proves their ingenuity. The soldiers, of course, had extra weapons and equipment; there was a great deal of baggage carried on a limited number of packhorses and by the unfortunate camp-followers.

The stark plan was to abandon Munster and travel immediately north to join forces with Hugh O'Neill, Earl of Tyrone and former commander-in-chief at Kinsale. He was believed to be in rebellion still in Ulster. Such a journey would involve a south–north traverse of the whole island of Ireland, against the grain of political and military conditions. From the very beginning, food would have to be captured from hard-pressed communities who would defend their resources.

O'Sullivan was accompanied on the march by his seventy-year-old uncle, Dermot of Dursey, and by a dispossessed chieftain, O'Conor Kerry, more ancient still. Carrying food for a single day, the convoy marched over twenty-four miles on New Year's Eve 1602. That their departure was not betrayed by spies is extraordinary, and it is tempting to imagine that Wilmot let them go in order to avoid a bloody confrontation, having already achieved his ends. The move was executed so swiftly that pursuit would have been futile.

NORTHWARDS

The modern road through Glengarriff weaves along the shore of Bantry Bay, then strikes inland and gradually uphill along the Owvane valley. In winter 2002, the re-enactment of O'Sullivan's March took this blistering tarmac. Led by a piper in pleasant sunshine, locals escorted the long-distance walkers out along the road, as if to ensure that no one doubled back. The original convoy travelled in this direction. They had assembled in the woods overnight and moved out in groups under cover of darkness, slipping along cattle tracks on the lower slopes of the foothills. With their departure, the remaining population of Beara was left at the mercy of Wilmot. In the tradition of victory, he savaged the peninsula. This sums up O'Sullivan's dilemma, and that of all guerrilla forces. His resistance had provoked an all-out attack by the Crown. When he chose to flee, his people were left defenceless to suffer the consequences.

During the day, they passed within reach of Carriganass Castle, built on a narrow ravine of the Owvane River. It was still in the hands of O'Sullivan's people, soon to surrender. Perhaps it represented a notional defence against pursuit. A hull of masonry today, with the exposed look of a nut cracked open, the castle stands on a shelf overlooking the river.

MUSKERRY

O'Sullivan was heading for the funnel of Keimaneigh (*Céim an Fhia*: Deer's Leap), a pass breaching the Shehy Mountains. Throughout history, the natural barriers of the landscape – mountains, rivers, bogs – separated peoples and events. Those barriers determined where and how journeys were made. Peaceful travel followed the easiest channels; illicit journeys tended towards the hills.[1]

The route probably did not thread the bed of the ravine, as the modern road does. Keimaneigh was first widened to take a coach in the 1830s. In O'Sullivan's time, the ravine would have been a bottleneck on the border of hostile terrain, threatened by ambush. Many of his neighbours had gone over to the Crown – some for want of alternative on the collapse of rebellion; some to improve their prospects; and some from an inborn tendency to defect.

I have walked that twenty-four-mile day in winter, with cushioned insoles, thermal underwear and Goretex weather-gear, and was glad of gravity to get me down the long, last, weary hill. The re-enactment went through the pass itself, which is lined with thickets of birch, hazel and ash, spoiled only by the bristling of sitka spruce. The rocks above the road were dark and dripping on New Year's Eve, 2002. The thinnest twigs of birch were jewelled with rain; they infused the gloom of evening with a delicate purple hue.

FIRST CAMPSITE

Wherever possible, O'Sullivan linked a series of holy places, adding a sense of pilgrimage to his journey. There was nothing new in this. Irish insurgents in the Elizabethan wars saw themselves not only as defending Ireland against the invader, but also as Catholics resisting heretics. This image was used in Europe, where the Counter Reformation was underway, and Ireland claimed assistance both for military reasons and on account of religious persecution.

❧ *Gougane Barra*

With time, certain journeys develop a seasoned twist that shapes the grain to what ought to have been. According to folklore, instead of the lowland route he had followed from Glengarriff, O'Sullivan went across all the hilltops of west Cork on that first day. It is plausible on the map and is the route a committed hill-walker would favour today. Ignoring the horses and the convoy, tradition ushers him down from the highest mountains in a mantle of rainbows, on a cushion of cloud, into the holy fastness of Gougane Barra, uniting soldier and saint in a triumph of Gaelic spirit. Against a powerful enemy, the Irish always lost the war, but the techniques of symbolic victory were fiercely honed. Other accounts, balking at the mountain, still steer O'Sullivan's men into Gougane Barra for prayers. But Philip O'Sullivan, nephew of Donal Cam, writing an account of the march, *Historiae Catholicae Iberniae Compendium*, does not mention the place at all. According to his terse note of that day, his uncle set up camp 'in Muskerry country, at a place which the locals call Augeris'.

An Teampaillín, the little church at Eachros, near Ballingeary, was the last place in which the marchers were to rest without disturbance. A tumbledown ruin today, it is tucked away in the fields beyond Cronin's farmyard (entrance by permission). The ground is soft in winter, easily churned by hooves, but with the look of good summer grazing. The church had no architectural interest, to judge by the fragment of wall and gable standing, but it has an eerie sense of sustained presence. An old ash tree grows within the walls with the venerable look of wood forced up through stone. Even in O'Sullivan's time, four hundred years ago, the church was in ruins. In that treacherous landscape, its hallowed ground symbolised sanctuary of some sort. A bivouac on holy ground was less likely to provoke the rage of rival factions.

People slumped to the ground in exhaustion at Eachros, wrapped in the *clóca*, the Irish mantle of homespun wool, so versatile in its simplicity that it could be used in numerous ways, making it a kind of mobile habitat. It was defined by Spenser, the Elizabethan poet, as a camouflage for thieves – although it became standard issue for English soldiers in Ireland.

At that early stage, ponies and people were still carrying possessions. No one abandons the sticks and rags of domestic order until forced to do so. There were probably old mantles for blankets and bedding. Some rawhide tents, very heavy, can be assumed for the leaders. Others would have looped a few rods in the ground and covered them with whatever possible – skins, mantles again, perhaps. There is an ancient tradition that shelters of this kind were roofed with 'scraws', lengths of vegetated topsoil stripped from the ground. Until recently, some houses were thatched in this manner.

Smoky fires were lit between stacked stones. The last thing they wanted was to flaunt their presence and provoke the locals. More than the threat of hostility, food occupied their thoughts. People had a consummate knowledge of berries, herbs and roots – of any soup, broth or potion possible. But it was winter and wartime. Philip O'Sullivan's report says they carried rations for one day – with the length of Ireland ahead of them. The potato was not yet in common use. It is unlikely that many of them had even seen one. Because of the ravages of war, oats may have been as valuable as the Spanish gold. Commentators have guessed at unleavened oatcakes as provisions, and the rough-churned butter which was a means of storing milk for the winter. That might conjure an image of the marchers around a bonfire scoffing homemade bread with lashings of country butter and some of the farmhouse cheeses for which west Cork is famous to-day. However, when they lost the *creacht* (the herd), in late December 1602, they lost virtually all means of subsistence.

Inevitably some of the refugees would have been carrying infants. If modern convoys are anything to go by, there must have been children, dressed in rags, bearing pathetic bundles. If so, the pressure of that winter's day was already taking its toll. For centuries, the ground has been used as a *cillín*, a graveyard for unbaptised children, stillborn infants, and probably for those denied burial elsewhere. This is the reason why such sites are left undisturbed in desolate privacy. The *cillín* is one of the deepest wounds in our identity. It leads down into Limbo, where unbaptised souls were shut away from eternal light and ignored by God forever.

The weather appears to have been stable in the early days of the march. It was to change dramatically. From detailed accounts of the Nine Years' War (1593–1603), we know that the winters were exceptionally severe. The period is sometimes described as a kind of mini-ice-age. A morning campsite in bad conditions is no place for a delicate constitution. Men grow rough on an ugly journey, in order to conceal their fears and weaknesses, be they soldiers, hunters, herders, refugees or mountaineers. Bones are stiff, wounds painful, the belly empty, the spirit low. Discipline barely overcomes failure of the will. The presence of women and children on O'Sullivan's march would not necessarily mollify the roughness. It could increase it, not just among the brutish, but also among those who understood the annihilation that lay in store for the weak. There must have been soldiers with O'Sullivan who felt that they were being slowed down, and that such a march was no place for non-combatants.

Military discipline does not inspire civilians. After a cold and hungry march, exhaustion takes over and most people stiffen into a stupor. Leadership is essential to rouse them to an effort. Unloading animals, getting them to grass where they can feed, caring for children, keeping watch in shifts – all are part of the effort that keeps a group together under desperate conditions. That O'Sullivan was a fine commander becomes obvious as the march goes on, but whether he was an inspiration to his general followers is less certain.

Small groups began to leak away from this point on. There is a trail of families stretching northwards to this day, who claim descent from those who left the march. Some of these claims may well be dubious, because west Cork names are widespread for many reasons. Certain families have carried the 'Beara' tag for generations. It is difficult to know whether or not it is genuine, as the tradition could have been assumed retrospectively for the best of motives.

In the morning, O'Sullivan lost his favourite horse, *An Chearc*, the Hen. The horse is thought to have been named for his high-stepping style, though it hardly seems a compliment – especially since the name is feminine and the horse is thought to have been a stallion. The event is not mentioned in the 'official' account, written much later by O'Sullivan's nephew, Philip, who was brought up in Spain. According to local folklore, *An Chearc* broke a leg while being led over boggy ground soon after leaving Eachros. People who know little about the marchers and their fate know all about the horse. Sometimes he plunges to his death in a deep hole, or more plausibly, he is shot after breaking a leg. The hole, *Poll na Circe*, is still pointed out.

Perhaps O'Sullivan was riding the horse at the time of the

accident and was tactfully dismounted by folklore? Hardly –
folk memory thrives on defect and would never be so generous. Anyway, there is no place as cold and exposed in the
morning as a horse's back. It is far easier to warm up and
loosen out on foot. The horse was probably loaded with baggage and being led by a horseboy. It is worth noting that we
do not know the names of any of O'Sullivan's followers, apart
from close family, Gaelic nobles such as O'Conor Kerry, and a
few senior officers who commanded their own men. We have
more personal detail about a horse that died on the second
day than we have about a thousand people. Normally, such
an imbalance would be the result of the snobbery of Gaelic
writers and historians who erased the common people from
the record, while a favourite horse or dog might get honourable mention. However, *An Chearc* is recorded only in folk
tradition. Since the story concerns a faithful animal with a
contradictory name, it was probably told to generations of
children, along with tales of Oisín's white horse and Fionn
Mac Cumhail's hunting dogs. We remember the tales of
childhood and we pass them on in turn.

In any case, it is hard to believe that the starving throng
would not have butchered the carcass and eaten it, as soldiers have always done (on Napoleon's retreat from Moscow,
for example). There is a sense of an elevated decision from
the top. Philip reports on later occasions that Donal Cam and
his uncle Dermot both abstained from horseflesh. In Ireland,
there was a traditional respect for horses – a sense that they
were not far removed from human status. That respect
would soon be vindicated.

Ballyvourney

Late that morning, they reached the village of Ballyvourney and stopped to visit the shrine of St Gobnait, famed for healing. Eighteen months earlier, Pope Clement VIII had marked this shrine with a special indulgence for those who prayed for the Church in the battle against heretics. There, in Philip's words, the soldiers 'gave vent to unaccustomed prayers, and made offerings, beseeching the saint for a happy journey'. The Ballyvourney saint had a way of ignoring prayers. For centuries, a one-eyed statue was kept in the care of the O'Herlihys. A cure for smallpox was traditionally associated with the wooden image of the saint. Its reputation suffered, however, when two of the custodians came down with smallpox.

Philip O'Sullivan Beare, the commentator, was ten or twelve years old and already in Spain when his uncle, Donal Cam, marched out of west Cork, never to return. Dermot O'Sullivan, the old man accompanying Donal, was actually Philip's father. Philip grew up to have a career in the Spanish navy and to become a colourful voice in Europe on behalf of Ireland. His strident excesses caused his counterparts to cringe. While his work is inaccurate in many areas, it seems reasonable to trust the practical details of his uncle's journey, although Philip never missed an opportunity to strike a heroic pose from the safety of the next generation.

The MacCarthys

The march moved on and ran into its first conflict. The attackers were the sons of Thady MacCarthy from the castle of

Carrigaphooca by the River Sullane, former allies of Donal Cam. Not only had they defected to the English, but they also kept the bribe which O'Sullivan had paid for their loyalty. To their indignation, he had attacked their castle and taken his money back. If it weren't for the underlying tragedy of dispossession and death, one might observe that many episodes of the period have that kind of cowboy quality.[2]

The attack on the march lasted four hours, with the Sons of Thady MacCarthy trailing the convoy, snapping viciously at its heels and scattering under fire. It is tempting to see them whooping in on fast ponies, snapping off shots and wheeling away. However, the musket was a hopelessly clumsy gun that took a long time to load and fire. As well as being smoky and inaccurate, it was prone to blowing up in the face of the musketeer. Guns were scarce and must have been major status symbols. Still, the shooting went on and on, as if the possession of weapons was the actual reason for the attack. Like a dog, a gun demands exercise.

O'Sullivan's troops were divided in two, with one section at the head of the march, the other guarding the rear, herding the civilians onwards. MacCarthy's sidekicks seized every chance to slip alongside and fire into the straggling mass before the soldiers headed them off. The attack would then recoup and press harder on the depleted rear. The civilians resembled nothing so much as the *creacht*, which had been lost. Burdened, helpless, hustled along, they must have heard the noise of muskets like the cracking of unseen whips behind their backs. The vanguard must have taken to wooded ground to give cover on the vulnerable flanks. A great deal of baggage was lost. Loads were shed by pack animals and by running fugitives who had carried their possessions nearly thirty miles already, up and over the Pass of Keimaneigh the previous day, hoping that the weight on their backs would be the makings of a new life somewhere to the north.

Suddenly, O'Sullivan wheeled his formation around, pulled his advance guard to the rear and attacked the Mac-Carthy forces head-on with doubled numbers. It was not as simple as it sounds. The tactic must have been hard to handle on the move and under fire. Some of the enemy was slain in the head-on clash, and the rest fled.

The convoy was attacked again by another faction of the MacCarthys, from Kilmeady Castle, near Millstreet, where O'Sullivan camped that night. It appears to have been a token flourish, the way a dog runs snarling to the gate when a bigger beast is safely past.

On that day also, O'Sullivan travelled twenty-four miles. Nothing had been eaten all day. They were left in no doubt as to local opinion. Throughout the night, a barrage of howls and yells raged in the darkness beyond the campsite. Sleeplessness was added to hunger. If there was any satisfaction to be had, it lay in knowing that the locals were sleepless too. No time was wasted on breakfast ....

The pattern was to continue. The country ahead was seething with fear and hostility in the aftermath of war. O'Sullivan had no option but to pick a way through the Munster hills, dodging from height to height, weaving north towards the Shannon. The dangerous valleys and plains had to be crossed too. There is no reference to local guides, but his Connacht mercenaries would have travelled this terrain before.

At the ford of Ballybahellagh on the River Allow, between Newmarket and Liscarroll, the next battle occurred. The Allow rises in the Mullaghareirk Hills on the Cork and

Limerick border and flows into the Blackwater to the west of
Mallow. An English garrison defended the ford, with Irish
support as usual. O'Sullivan was outnumbered, according to
Philip. Stafford's English account has the balance the other
way round (*Pacata Hibernia*). A hard-fought battle ensued,
'with red-hot balls from both sides'. It lasted about an hour.
Philip identified the opposing forces in black and white,
hammering home, for a European audience, the heroic struggle between the faithful and the heretics:

> In this fight four of the Catholics fell; the royalists lost more,
> many were wounded, and perhaps more would have perished,
> although they were superior in numbers, were it not that the
> Catholics, through want and weariness were unable to pursue
> them. The Catholics having buried their dead and in turns
> carrying the wounded in military litters, accomplished a march of
> thirty miles that day ....

Obviously, it was not in Philip's interest to acknowledge that
most of the royalists were also Irish Catholics. But he was
caught between the conflicting need to tell Catholic Europe
of the fate endured by the Irish at the hands of heretics,
while at the same time avenging himself on the Gaelic clans
who had turned their weapons on the people of west Cork.
The stigma has long since vanished, and the anniversary
march of 2002–3 was welcomed everywhere by the descendants of original enemies. Four hundred years later, the same
family names are found in the same areas all along the route.

 # THE GOLDEN VALE

Almost eighty miles had been covered in three extraordinary
days, and O'Sullivan had reached a point identified in the

Annals of the Four Masters as Ardpatrick, in Co. Limerick. This is also a holy place, another rough bead in O'Sullivan's rosary. The heather-brown of the Ballyhoura Mountains ranked behind it emphasises Ardpatrick's claim to be the highest green hill in Ireland. This grassy dome has a long history of significance. A church on top, one of the high points of early Christianity, was replaced by the monastery and tower now slumped in ruins. It is easy to see why the early Church would choose such a landmark, dominating the pastoral plains of Limerick, some of the richest land in Ireland. If anything, Ardpatrick suggests a stack of this lush land heaped up high to show how much there is to spare. What did the starving men of west Cork, raised on rock, think of this magnificent ground as they stumbled through the grass, scraping up roots to cook for soup? The land may have been wild at the time, after a decade of unrest, and perhaps they were spared that vision of the unattainable.

'On the following day,' Philip writes poignantly, 'they refreshed themselves with cresses and water and hurried along in a direct route before sunrise.' Today, more than any other place in Ireland, that direct route is awash with milk. Philip, who worked in Latin, actually wrote *cum se leguminibus et aqua refecissent*. It was the translator, nudged into association perhaps by that *aqua* who narrowed the focus to watercress, associated in Gaelic literature with hermits for its cleanness and ascetic flavour. The image of the multitude setting forth across the Golden Vale, fortified by sprigs of cress after days of hunger, has taken a powerful hold in a culture eager for symbols of pure courage in adversity. Out of pity, we can only hope that Philip was exaggerating as he often was, or that *cum leguminibus* might have included root vegetables of some kind, although potatoes would not be widely grown in Ireland for another forty years.

The crossing of the open plain between the Ballyhoura Mountains and Slieve Felim to the northeast would be the most exposed section of the march so far. Controlled by Maurice Fitzgerald, the Earl of Desmond (known as the White Knight), the route passes near the present towns of Kilfinnane and Emly. The shifting alliances of the Irish and the ferocious consequences of such change are crystallised in the career of the Geraldine White Knight. His military base was at Hospital, so named from an earlier foundation of the Knights Hospitallers. After sustained resistance, Fitzgerald had submitted to English rule in May 1600, and was away campaigning against rebel Irish when O'Sullivan stumbled into his territory. Despite the White Knight's absence, the area was heavily defended by an assortment of soldiers and local mercenaries, particularly of the Gibbons clan. The mix was thickened by men from Limerick city.

They must have made a considerable force, because they hammered and tore at O'Sullivan throughout the day, 'charging boldly in front, rear, and baggage which was carried in the middle, attacking all at once.' The Sons of Thady Mac-Carthy were only an irritation compared to this. The running battle lasted eight hours, and the gunfire from both sides was at times so heavy that the opposing sides could not see each other. That detail reads like a flourish from Philip's experience of war in the Spanish navy rather than the discharge of muskets on a windy plain in January; but there is no reason to doubt the claim that O'Sullivan could neither carry off his wounded nor bury his dead.

FOOD RAID

Despite heavy losses, they covered twenty miles that dreadful day, to camp at Solohead, *Sulchóid*, where Brian Boru had routed the Danes of Limerick AD 968. The night appears to have been the coldest so far. The starving soldiers foraged for plants and roots and huddled around the fires that drew attention to their presence. Their wounds and losses must have stripped away all reserve and left them with a single option. In the morning, they attacked a tower on the prominent mound of Donohill. The local O'Dwyers defended it.

The first to break in devoured whatever food they could lay hands on, while the rest fed on 'meal, beans and barley grains like cattle'. Donohill was always a centre for milling, and quantities of grain must have been stored in the tower against the threat of a starving army. There was probably only enough for a bellyful for the lucky few. The entire country was in the grip of hunger and it is unlikely that Donohill was a treasury of golden grain. Barley can indeed be eaten raw. It is still customary to rub ears of corn between the palms while walking the fields, to blow the husks away and to chew the grain into a floury paste. If the whisker is swallowed, it feels like a fishbone in the throat. Twenty miles were covered again that day, and maybe those who had hurled food down their gullets regretted the lack of restraint. Raw food passes through a starving stomach like shot through a musket barrel.

It took two more days to reach a crossing point on the Shannon. The numbers were reduced by a third already. Apart from the dead, and the wounded who had been left behind, others had melted away or failed to keep up. The Irish countryside was by no means deserted at the time. The population is put at a tentative 1.4 million in 1600, though the aftermath of war, with famine and plague, was reducing numbers, particularly in Munster. It is hard to imagine that stragglers on O'Sullivan's journey could have put down roots without local support, or at least tolerance. Individual acts of kindness must have occurred, but they were not recorded; there is nothing to relieve that baleful sense of a country hounding its own outcasts, grinding them down to skeletons and ghosts.

So far, the route had threaded the logic of the hills, while they lasted. It was by no means a random, reeling flight, but a sequence of strategic dashes and sorties. Just as the Pass of Keimaneigh breached the Shehy Mountains, an ancient route led north through the Slieve Felim range, avoiding the hostile plains of Tipperary and Limerick to the east and west. That this was a major passage is reflected not only in the journey of O'Sullivan, but also in the routes of O'Donnell and Patrick Sarsfield, who passed in different directions through the Slieve Felim village of Hollyford on illicit missions, at opposite ends of that century. In O'Sullivan's case, there was no escaping confrontation; the heat was on. The idiom is apt because, on the morning of 6 January, in Philip's words, 'a storm of red-hot balls blazed on O'Sullivan as he advanced. This was a daily salutation with which the enemy honoured him; a farewell as they drew off at night; a greeting as they turned up in the morning.'

Chieftains and leaders had to put on a bold show of allegiance to the Crown in order not to fall victim themselves. But zeal in the execution of harsh duty has always been a characteristic of power, even when it has just changed sides.

Any attempt to hack their way onwards to the east of the Shannon would be suicidal. The Crown stronghold of King's County (Offaly) lay just ahead, fraught with garrisons and showers of molten lead. Crossing the River Shannon made no geographical sense; it was a political and a military choice. Connacht would be more Gaelic, less hostile. In choosing that route, O'Sullivan was leading many of his hired soldiers home. Perhaps they had no intention of being led anywhere else. Perhaps they were leading him.

He would be repeating, almost exactly in reverse, Red Hugh O'Donnell's march south from Ballymote in Sligo, a year before, en route to Kinsale. Maps of the two marches show an identical kink, the same sidestep across the Shannon midway. O'Donnell, in his pillaging of the route, had done no one any favours, least of all his own troops, slinking back in disorder a short while later.

SHANNON CROSSING

Brought up close to the route, in Roscommon, I had heard echoes of the events in primary school – O'Donnell going down, O'Sullivan coming up. It was like being tuned between two radio-stations, a circus parade in one ear, a funeral march in the other. The two journeys, so similar in itinerary, mark the high and the low points of the Nine Years' War – triumph and desolation.

O'Sullivan tackled the Shannon just north of Portumna. This point was within reach of Redwood Castle, home of the MacEgans, *Clann Mhic Aodhagáin*, a long-established family noted for scholarship and learning. For centuries, the MacEgans had been academic figures in Gaelic culture, professors of the Brehon laws to all Ireland. Students came to them as to an academy. Cairbre MacEgan and his son Flann were held in high regard in the Gaelic world. If O'Sullivan had any luck at all, they could be expected to appreciate his credentials. Unfortunately, the MacEgans were in a royalist phase. Donogh, son of Cairbre and brother of Flann, was the local Queen's Sheriff. To many later observers, this was like being Sheriff of Nottingham in the time of Robin Hood.

All boats had been withdrawn at Donogh's order from the Shannon, and the ferrymen were warned 'under the severest penalties' not to carry O'Sullivan over. That was already a severe penalty on the boatmen, with hundreds of passengers on the horizon and O'Sullivan still carrying the Spanish gold. He was caught in a trap, his back to the river, the expanse of Lough Derg downstream, and military extinction guaranteed to the north.

The river was wider then than now; drainage has deepened and narrowed it – and presumably speeded up the current. The Redwood bank, still boggy today, was a sprawling marsh. A little further back, it was heavily wooded. The Beara men went to ground in a clearing on 7 January. They

❧ The MacEgans

Hereditary professors of Brehon law to the local O'Kennedys, the MacEgans would continue to be reputable Gaelic scholars, and a few years later the work of the Four Masters would be brought here to Flann MacEgan for an *imprimatur*. This is a little eerie: the annals were principally compiled by Michael O'Clery, a former pupil of the MacEgans, and the work would also contain an account of the events that were to befall O'Sullivan at MacEgan hands. These tangled strands hint at the complex connections and contradictions of the Gaelic world.

dug a defensive trench and built a barrier of felled trees. *Gort na gCapall* (field of the horses) is flanked by an acre or so of dense shrubbery today: mainly ash, heavy with ivy and overgrown at the base by whitethorn and briar. Doubtful whether anything growing there now is even a hundred years old, and yet the imagination seizes on the trees at once as O'Sullivan's lair. A pair of old pylons carries a power line across the river at this point today.

Philip credits his father, Dermot of Dursey, with the idea of building a boat. Competition set in. The O'Malleys of Mayo reckoned that they could build a better boat than the Cork men could. Twelve horses were killed and skinned. The flesh was eaten by the ravenous horde, except, as Philip insists, by his own father and by his uncle, Donal Cam.

The leaders might have had a private supply of food with them, of course. They certainly had servants and grooms, just as each mounted soldier had one, or perhaps two, horseboys to look after equipment. A supply of food for the leader and senior officers is not unlikely and would explain their consistent energy and drive, and also the survival of the two elderly figures, Dermot of Dursey and O'Conor Kerry. The old men would have spent much of the journey so far on horseback. That would change. Horses were about to become very scarce.

The O'Sullivan boat began upside down as a willow frame, made of poles stuck in the ground, the tips bent in to meet each other and tied with cord. (In Ireland, boat building of this kind was traditionally done with hazel rather than willow.) Crossbeams, planks and seats strengthened the frame. It was covered outside with the skins of eleven horses, and then equipped with oars. The boat was twenty-six feet (almost eight metres) long. In other words, it was the same length as a full-size currach, but a foot and a half broader and a bit deeper too.

The O'Malleys were left with a single skin for their boat, whether by design or by disdain, we don't know. They made a circular, top-heavy coracle that sounds very like an egg-basket. 'It was covered with the skin of one horse drawn over the bottom.' Ten of the O'Malleys got into it and drowned in the middle of the river. The episode reads like a management-training game gone wrong. Philip is probably being spiteful. River boats of this kind were not uncommon, but no one would have attempted ten passengers.

The O'Sullivan boat, after two days' work in the secrecy of the wood, was carried down to the river at night and began to ferry people across at the rate of 'thirty armed men at a time … the horses swimming and tied to the poop'. Most of the armed men had been ferried over by daybreak.

Forty soldiers remained behind on the Redwood bank, in ambush, to protect the women and the baggage. Unaware of the armed guard, Donogh MacEgan attacked at this point, killing horseboys and driving 'the terror-stricken women into the river'. The soldiers sprang out of hiding and killed Donogh, along with fifteen of his men. It would take enormous charity to regret the Sheriff's fate. Commentators, including the Four Masters, all lament the shame that had fallen on the MacEgans through Donogh's folly.

Crowds of hostile locals had gathered on both banks by then. As the rearguard was brought over in haste after the Sheriff's death, the boat was swamped. Fortunately they were close to the bank and able to float it again. It is difficult to imagine heaving that weight out of the water to empty it.

Presumably they held off the mob with the threat of musket fire, but it must have taken a miracle to keep powder dry in such conditions. In the panic, some members of the party were left behind. The account does not pursue their fate.

Crossing at the same point in a smaller currach, in January 2003, we found a very strong current, increased by a northeast wind. The river is deeper and faster now than it was in O'Sullivan's time. A pair of west Cork oarsmen rowed our currach, one an O'Sullivan. They battled fiercely upstream in order to cut across the current and lunge at a sharp tangent for the opposite shore. A powerful effort and sharp judgement were required on each journey in order to land at the right spot, slotting the prow of the currach in between stands of reeds at the bank. Two passengers per trip were carried, and it was difficult to imagine increasing this to four. There appears to have been little rain during O'Sullivan's journey

---

∾ The Boat

That such a boat could have achieved so much is nothing less than miraculous. Thirty armed soldiers is an impossible load for a makeshift craft, unless shoals of them were towed behind it. There is a hint that some of the horseboys swam the river. On reaching the opposite shore, O'Sullivan had two hundred and eighty armed men in his command. In that case, at least a dozen journeys over would have been required, and the same number back. Given the width and flow of the river, it borders on the miraculous. Or the fictional: Philip had the instincts of a novelist rather than a historian. But the timetable of the march left little room for creative tampering, and a contemporary English account confirms the horsehide boats. Certainly the marchers were transported across the river in that period of two days. Philip had a career in the Spanish navy and understood boats in detail. So too would his audience, and he gave measurements that exposed his case to scrutiny.

so far, and the shallow current would have been slow-flowing. A prevailing wind, from the southwest and against the current, would also have helped.

The O'Maddens of the Connacht bank welcomed the 2003 re-enactment with tea and sandwiches in a riverside pub. Their ancestors had greeted Donal Cam with a volley of lead in 1603. The west Cork men plundered a local village on that occasion, where they feasted on raw beans and grain, swilled down with stolen ale. The pursuit was so heated that O'Sullivan was forced to abandon wounded and exhausted men. Having leapt the widest river to gain the staunchest province, he was entitled now to expect a reprieve. Philip's mention of beer suggests the point in heroic myth where a climax is marked by feasting. But O'Sullivan's greatest trials were still to come.

 # Aughrim

Diverting west of the River Suck where it joins the Shannon to shape the symmetry of south Roscommon, he marched through Co. Galway. On 10 January, at the hill of Aughrim, his famished force was blocked by an army of cavalry and infantry. Drawn up to meet him were two troops of horse and five companies of foot. Bands of scavengers skulked on the sidelines. This far superior force, arrayed in battle order, was commanded by Captain Henry Malby. Second-in-command was Thomas Burke, whose brother had been knighted for bravery on the English side at Kinsale a year earlier. O'Sullivan too had distinguished himself in that battle, on the Irish side. Yet another Crown-supporting Burke – Richard – also assisted Malby in command.

The waiting soldiers were armed and armoured, fed and rested. Flaunting banners, trumpets and drums, they were an unnerving sight. The Irish vanguard scattered in appal. O'Sullivan addressed his men in one of the showpiece speeches that resound throughout the annals of Irish rhetoric. Whether he spoke as reported, or Philip added eloquence at leisure; whether it was addressed to two hundred and eighty horrified men, or simply to a clutch of officers, the speech has a backs-to-the-wall, Faith-of-our-Fathers resonance that can still move the heart four centuries later at the thought of a famished remnant facing an army of well-fed troops.

> Since our desperate fortunes have left us here without means or country, wives or children to fight for, the struggle with our enemies before us now is for our bare lives; we have nothing else that we can lose .... In God's eternal name I ask you, men, will you not rather fall gloriously in battle, avenging your blood, than die like brute cattle in a cowardly fight? Our ancestors would never seek to avoid an honourable death. Let us follow in the footsteps of our sires: there is no other salvation. See around you the country is bare of woods or bog; there is no concealment; the people of these parts offer us no aid. Roads and passes are blocked, even if we had strength to fly. Our only hope is in our own courage, and the strength of our own arms ....

A note of manic confidence then:

> Remember that everywhere hitherto, enemies who attacked us were routed by the Divine Mercy. Victory is the gift of God ....

As the opposite had, in fact, been the case, he moved swiftly to conclude:

> Fear not this worthless mob: they are not men of such fame as we, nor used to fight as we are ....

Versions of this punch line have resounded in the ears of

soldiers down through the centuries, before and after O'Sullivan. No doubt, the Celts in their time used it against the Romans and vice versa.

Malby's cavalry was charging even as O'Sullivan deployed his men. A second column closed on him in a pincer movement. He raced over boggy ground to gain a wooded rise. Forty musketeers protected the rear. Malby's charging horsemen were forced to dismount in the swamp. Pikes swinging, they joined their own infantry in the attack. Meanwhile, O'Sullivan's rearguard of musketeers was overwhelmed by the enemy column, and fourteen of the Irish were killed. In a sudden move, O'Sullivan flung his entire force around to confront this threat. We have seen him do that before. This defiance unnerved the enemy, who were expecting an easy rout. They may have assumed that the Irish were already in retreat. O'Sullivan's musketeers shot down eleven, in exchange for the fourteen lost. A number of the attackers broke ranks and fled. There is a tight-lipped hint that some of O'Sullivan's men pulled out too. It was hand-to-hand fighting then, with spears, pikes and swords: stabbing, flailing, chopping.

Immediately, the outnumbered Irish fastened on the opposing leaders in a do-or-die attack. They went straight for the top. Malby was chopped down by O'Houlihan and O'Murrough (the Four Masters claim he was killed by Donal Cam); Malby's senior officer, Richard Burke, was hacked to death by Maurice O'Sullivan and two others, each strike described in detail. Thomas Burke was left in command. He had himself and his armour hoisted onto his horse and he rode urgently away.

It is impossible to stall such ferocity once unleashed.

Fighting continued until the English army, leaderless, re-treated to the nearby garrison. They were chased by the Irish – in particular, it seems, by those who had wobbled earlier and were keen now to retrieve their honour. This faction is awarded a special sting of contempt. The field was strewn with dead English and with Queen's Irish. O'Sullivan had some of their fallen banners gathered. He scattered the rabble who were plundering his baggage under cover of the battle, and he continued northwards.

It is claimed that he lost no more than the original fourteen while a hundred of Malby's force were killed. Such figures are rhetorical propaganda, but there is no doubt that the Battle of Aughrim, 1603, was a stunning victory for O'Sullivan. Eighty-eight years later, in 1691, during the Williamite war, another battle was to take place on the same ground. Saint-Ruth, leader of the Jacobites, on whom native Irish hopes were pinned, was decapitated by a cannon ball. Over seven thousand Jacobites were killed, and the Battle of Aughrim, 1691, became the bloodiest battle fought in Ireland.

The flush of victory was soon to fade from O'Sullivan's column, which had not a moment's rest after Aughrim. There were many wounded, and while the soldiers had managed to re-arm themselves from the debris of the battlefield, their defiance could only arouse greater resistance from surrounding garrisons. In order to outflank this threat, O'Sullivan carried out a twenty-mile march into the night through O'Kelly country, the beginning of an extraordinary loop to the west. His destination was Leitrim, where the rebel chieftain, O'Rourke of Breifne, still held out. Although close at hand, Breifne could be reached in safety only by a hook-shaped detour via the Curlew Mountains, which would double back into Leitrim from the west.

The next encounter is almost embarrassing in its pathos. Approaching Glinsk, a village of the MacDavitts, after a snowy night march, O'Sullivan's men tried to pass themselves off as an English column, displaying the Aughrim banners and beating the captured drums. They must have presented a dreadful spectacle – starving, dishevelled, bloody, flaunting the stolen colours, like ghosts of the hundred slain. The wooing of Glinsk was an attempt to fool the MacDavitts and to lay hands on unprotected food. It cannot have been a spontaneous flourish, because they had obviously carried drums and banners all night through the bogs as winter closed in around them and exhausted people fell by the wayside. Maybe they hoped to be ahead of the bad news of their own arrival. The hungry locals were not fooled. With jeers rather than weapons, they drove off their starving countrymen who, the previous day, had routed a royalist army in a savage welter of blood. As if he were chasing stray animals, MacDavitt harassed them northwards, so that they could not lay their hands on a scrap of food all day.

Covering another twenty miles or so, O'Sullivan seemed to have shaken off the pursuit. The convoy stopped for the night on high ground beyond the present town of Ballinlough. As soon as the campfires had been lit on the sodden ground and bodies had sunk to rest, they realised that an attack was being prepared in the darkness behind them. Banking up the campfires, they slipped away, just as they had done in Glengarriff, eleven days earlier. Now they were little more than a handful of refugees, of whom only about sixty were capable of fighting. The flurries of snow had given way to rain so heavy that 'they were scarcely able to bear the weight of their soaking clothes'. They became hopelessly lost in woodland during the night and covered no more than four miles. MacDavitt, who had set up the earlier ambush, caught up during the morning, and they were forced to draw up a ragged formation and drive him off.

There was a brief remission then, as if extremity had reached such a pitch that it could only relent. In the breathing space, the soldiers managed to feed themselves on the carcasses of two horses, and to bind their bare feet with scraps of rawhide. The two senior O'Sullivans again refused horseflesh, and again there is an eerie sense of dignity asserting itself and being seen to do so.

They slept that night undisturbed – hardly worth disturbing what remained of them. Afterwards, they wandered on and became scattered. It is as if they were sleepwalking, or blundering in circles on unknown ground. It has been pointed out that their perception at this stage would have been a kind of waking nightmare and that descriptions given years later would reflect that confusion. Rain and snow fell on endless muck, but the unremitting opposition of their own countrymen must have been the bitterest element of all. O'Sullivan continued his obsessive pace because if momentum were allowed to flag for a heartbeat, there might be no moving on again. The pace did not allow opposition to build ahead of him; no sooner had word reached his enemies of his approach than he was looming out of the rain and lurching past.

✳ Co. Roscommon

On the twelfth night of the march, O'Sullivan found himself with only a dozen men on a wooded hillside. Groups and individuals stumbled along behind in the darkness, some doomed to death as a result, others to wander further and further astray. The Connacht mercenaries, *buannachta*, must have melted homewards by then – those who had survived. One can only hope that they were paid. Soldiers were not hired individually, but delivered by their own leaders, operating like military subcontractors.

A large bonfire was lit on the hillside as a signal to the stragglers. It drew in some locals as well. For once, they were friendly. They even brought a present of food to O'Sullivan – a token probably, as there is no sense of riotous feasting. The locals also spread a story to the garrison that the fire had been lit by woodcutters. The garrison was based at Boyle, just south of Lough Key, blocking the shortest route to Leitrim. O'Sullivan remained where he was that day. Then, to outflank the military, he forced a night march through the Curlew Mountains and north of Lough Arrow, adding a final loop to the journey.

Today, the motorway to Sligo skirts the Curlews in a disdainful stride that reduces this once-crucial barrier between Connacht and Ulster to an undulation, a drop in the gears from fifth to fourth. Above the road, there is a striking sculpture in ragged steel of a chieftain on horseback – an Irish Apache – that gives a flash of what the landscape may once have been. On the margin of the European road, the mounted warrior represents an Irish triumph at the Battle of the Curlews, 1599, when the Nine Years' War was going well.

The wind whistles through the steel; rust gathers like dried blood. However battered it becomes, it cannot quite reflect O'Sullivan's convoy passing by. They were without horses by then.

Fifteen miles remained to the castle of O'Rourke of Breifne, now Leitrim village on the banks of the Shannon. The account focuses on the venerable chieftain, O'Conor Kerry, whose stamina so far had been inspiring. After the halt of the previous day, his legs refused to carry him. They were lacerated with wounds, encrusted with sores and blisters. He addressed his feet with a tragicomic speech, straight from Cervantes or a subplot of Shakespeare, and hammered them against the ground to show them who was boss. Then he got up and marched with the rest.

 ## Co. Leitrim

In that confused terrain, a guide mysteriously appeared. He is described as a cross between a druid and an angel. The image probably embodies the amazement of the wanderers at any kind of assistance, compounded years later by the imagination of a young listener in a different culture. They were in friendly territory now, within the ambit of O'Rourke of Breifne. At the last moment, a rescuer appeared, and the episode is presented in the surreal glow of that perception. That is to be kind to Philip O'Sullivan, whose work was unfortunately prone to excesses, both of gullibility and of guile. It was not beyond him to conjure divine intervention.

During the night, they passed through the village of Knockvicar where they were able to warm themselves and even buy some food. By a strange irony, the only venue on

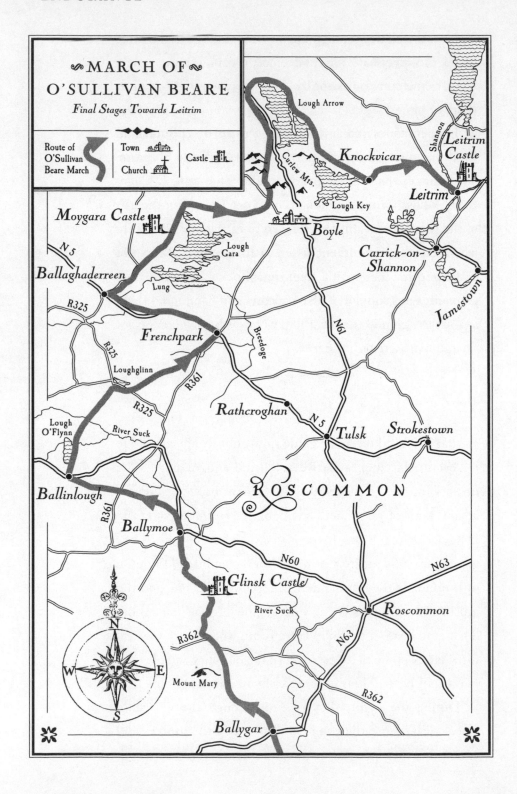

MARCH OF O'SULLIVAN BEARE
Final Stages Towards Leitrim

Route of O'Sullivan Beare March | Town | Church | Castle

Lough Arrow

Knockvicar

Shannon

Leitrim Castle

Curlew Mts.

Leitrim

Lough Key

Moygara Castle

Boyle

Carrick-on-Shannon

N5

Ballaghaderreen

Lough Gara

Jamestown

R325

Lung

Frenchpark

Breedoge

N61

R325

Loughglinn

R361

R325

Rathcroghan

N5

Tulsk

Strokestown

Lough O'Flynn

River Suck

Ballinlough

ROSCOMMON

R361

Ballymoe

N60

N63

Glinsk Castle

River Suck

Roscommon

R362

Mount Mary

N63

N

W   E

S

Ballygar

R362

the 2003 march which failed, by an oversight, to welcome the walkers was the same Knockvicar. Perhaps once was enough to rise to the occasion. A blind old nag was procured, its spine a rack of bones, and O'Conor Kerry was mounted upon him 'without bridle or saddle' – an image closer to the truth at that stage than the defiant warrior bone-welded to his horse on the rim of the Curlews just behind.

In the morning, the guide pointed out O'Rourke's castle in the distance and left with two hundred gold pieces O'Sullivan had given him without being asked. So, the real and terrible journey concluded, like a fable, with symbols of generosity and trust. In Philip's words:

> They reached Leitrim fort about eleven o'clock, being then reduced to 35, of whom 18 were armed … and one was a woman …. Some followed in twos and threes. I am astonished that Dermot O'Sullivan, my father, an old man near 70, and the woman of delicate sex, were able to go through these toils, which youths in the flower of age and height of their strength were unable to endure. O'Rourke received O'Sullivan with most honourable hospitality, giving directions to have his sick cured, and all necessaries supplied …. And he would have succoured O'Sullivan had he delayed longer there.

It is a pity not to have more information on those who arrived with O'Sullivan: the faithful thirty-five – particularly the mysterious woman. There may be any number of reasons for her anonymity, the most likely being lower-class station, so that she would not have merited identification by an aristocratic author. But some have scented intrigue: a lover accompanying Donal Cam while his wife remained hidden in the Eagle's Nest high among the Caha Mountains, awaiting escape to Spain. It is a spurious theory, but it lends itself to romantic fiction. Others assumed the lady to be Philip's mother, the wife of Dermot of Dursey. An inscription on a plaque at the ruins of O'Rourke's castle in Leitrim village actually makes this assumption. However, this is no longer credited, and Philip's account makes it clear that his mother had remained in Beara.

Donal Cam O'Sullivan was not a man to delay. Within days, he was on his way again, at the head of a renewed force, marching to join O'Neill who was a hundred miles and several flooded rivers away. But O'Neill was in extremity. Unaware that Queen Elizabeth had just died, he surrendered miserably, on his knees, before her emissary in March 1603. The Nine Years' War was over.

O'Neill, Earl of Tyrone, received a pardon. O'Conor Kerry was reinstated on his own lands. O'Rourke of Breifne, in rebellion to the last, died within the year. There was, and would be, no pardon for Donal Cam O'Sullivan. His cousin Owen, the Queen's O'Sullivan, became chieftain of Beara. Donal Cam escaped to Spain, where he was welcomed with honour and a pension and was proclaimed 'Count of Birhaven', to the chagrin of the English court. Years later, he was stabbed to death as a bystander at a duel fought, in a final irony, for his honour and reputation.

❧ Duel

Philip, defending the honour of his uncle, Donal Cam, got into a duel with one John Bathe, to whom money had been lent. Donal Cam, the innocent observer, was stabbed to death in the quarrel. Don Philippo, as the historian was known, remained unharmed. A born survivor, he outlived sixteen brothers and sisters.

# LEADERSHIP

O'Sullivan's March obviously resembles other military expeditions notorious for their hardship, but it also suggests certain journeys of exploration during which adversity whittled down the numbers, paring the flesh away from a central figure, as if to expose the very idea of leadership in all its desolate rags. In Beara, the herd on which O'Sullivan depended had been lost in a single battle. His most vulnerable followers were abandoned in the woods of Glengarriff. His favourite horse was cut out from under him on the second day. Soldiers were chopped down around him in batches. His people deserted, or were starved into disappearance.

Was he a brave and distinguished leader, the charismatic figure that folklore reveres, or simply a running man protected by hired soldiers? When his own castle at Dunboy, near Castletownbere, had been besieged by the Lord President of Munster in June of the previous year, he had failed to come to the rescue of its defenders. They were wiped out to a man after a dramatic stand, although O'Sullivan himself was no more than a few miles away, with additional troops. His refusal to respond is often interpreted as a callous, if not cowardly, failure.

It can also be argued that a mistake was made in leaving Munster, instead of continuing guerrilla warfare in the mountains. But from the moment the decision was taken, it was carried through with unswerving commitment. O'Sullivan still believed in Hugh O'Neill, Earl of Tyrone, strategist and driving force of the Nine Years' War, and he was marching north to join forces with him. Nothing deflected him from that purpose, not even the dreadful toll on his people.

III

POWER JOURNEYS:
KINGS & QUEENS

4 MEDB AND THE CATTLE-RAID OF COOLEY

(A Journey in the Iron Age)

A t the core of Táin Bó Cuailnge is a journey – a cattle-raiding quest that sundered Ireland nearly two thousand years ago.

An epic of the pagan Iron Age, the Táin tells of an army that marched from Roscommon in the west midlands to Carlingford in northeast Ulster, in order to capture the great brown bull of the Cooley Mountains.

There were challenges, battles and betrayals along the way. Pagan gods haunted the journey, flogging the action like angry ghosts; but the outcome hinged on human character – on jealousy, greed, loyalty and courage.

Queen Medb (Maeve) of Connacht assembled an army to

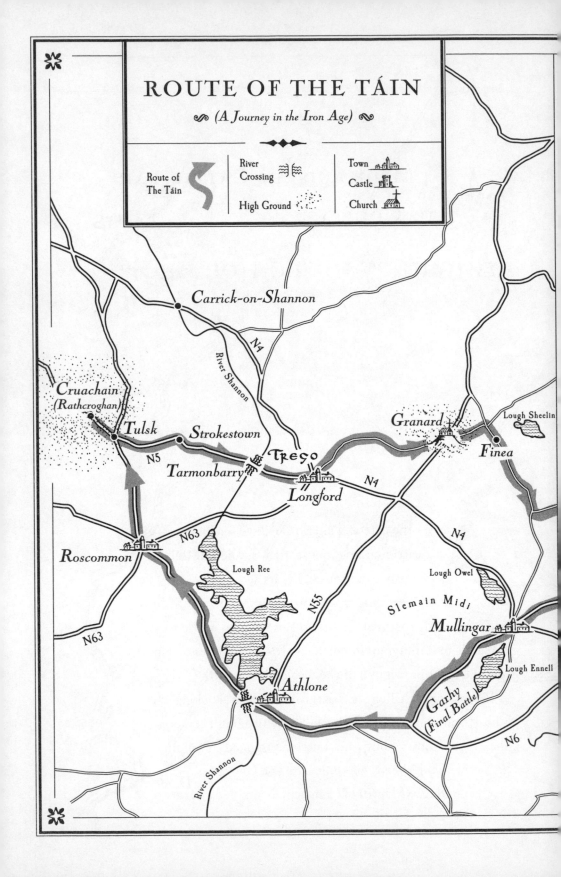

ROUTE OF THE TÁIN

(A Journey in the Iron Age)

Route of The Táin   River Crossing   Town

High Ground   Castle

Church

Carrick-on-Shannon

N4

River Shannon

Cruachain
(Rathcroghan)

Tulsk   Strokestown

N5   Tarmonbarry   Trego

Longford

Granard

Lough Sheelin

Finea

N4

Roscommon   N63

Lough Ree

N55

Lough Owel

Slemain Midi

N4

Mullingar

N63

Lough Ennell

Athlone

Garhy
(Final Battle)

N6

River Shannon

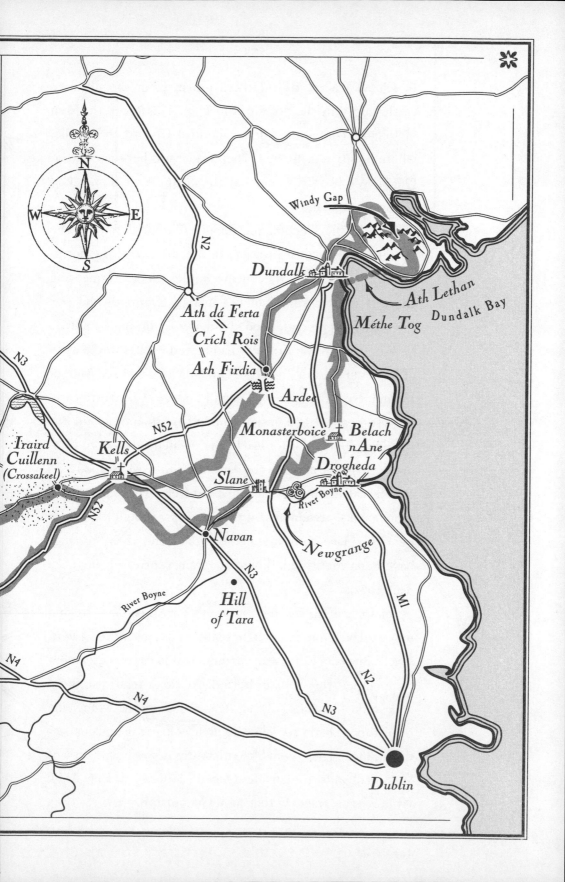

Windy Gap

Dundalk

Ath Lethan

Méthe Tog Dundalk Bay

N2

Ath dá Ferta

Crích Rois

Ath Firdia

Ardee

N3

N52

Monasterboice

Belach nAne

Iraird Cuillenn (Crossakeel)

Kells

Drogheda

Slane

River Boyne

Navan

Newgrange

N52

River Boyne

N3

Hill of Tara

M1

N4

N2

N4

N3

Dublin

march on Ulster, the northern province, in the ultimate cattle-raid – the theft of the primal bull. Her forces, the Men of Ireland, contained a detachment of Ulstermen in exile, whose loyalty was divided. Their leader was her secret lover. Queen Medb's army crossed the Shannon and marched across the midlands.

The heroic Cuchulainn, deeply flawed, defended the Ulster border against invasion. In the absence of the northern army, he faced the enemy hordes alone, tormenting them from the fringes of the march. Eventually he was forced to fight his childhood friend, Ferdia, in single combat.

When this private tragedy had played itself out, the army of Ulster arrived in pursuit of Queen Medb and the Men of Ireland. Near the shore of Lough Ennell, in Co. Westmeath, the last great battle erupted. It ended in a shameful rout. But the brown bull of Ulster had been captured and sent to Connacht. An image of death and darkness, the beast escaped ....

The cattle-raiding epic of ancient Ireland has seeped into schoolbooks, roadmaps, brochures. Its ringforts, earth mounds, place names, standing stones and river crossings have been identified. There are Táin centres, Táin trails, Táin towns.

In spite of all the fuss, we don't own this Táin. Ireland may well be grounded in it, but most of us have never read it. The Romans in Europe are far more real to us than their contemporaries, the Celts in Ireland. We don't recognise these ancestors. The tribes of the Táin are just on the wrong side of history, a little too close to archaeology for personal acquaintance. They seem like caricatures of myth with crowns and headbands: the envious Queen Medb, weak King Ailill, virile Fergus, tragic Ferdia, loyal Cuchulainn.

Hard for children to imagine Cuchulainn striding the land in sandals and tunic with a huge hub-cap of a shield; hard too to visualise flamboyant war camps in place of the grocery shops of Granard and Ardee; harder still to see Queen Medb as commander-in-chief, ploughing along in her chariot, up to the axle in muck. And yet, the story at the core of the Táin is as dramatic in many ways as any of the classic odysseys of the distant past.

THE ROUTE

Táin Bó Cuailnge comes storming off the written page, swaggering along the country roads, out of Roscommon, over the Shannon, through Longford, Meath and Louth. The trail of Queen Medb's cattle-raid is stitched in place by signposts among the wild grasses of the long mile – the roadside verge. The entire route of the Iron Age journey can be plotted in the modern landscape, with virtually every campsite of Medb's army identifiable. The Táin is a local journey on a national scale, its hoof-prints and wheel-ruts gouged into familiar landmarks. It fords the River Shannon, ploughs the mud of Dundalk Bay, climbs the Cooley Mountains, and staggers back onto the Central Plain. The Táin campaign covered in all about three hundred and fifty miles (five hundred and sixty kilometres) from Rathcroghan in Co. Roscommon to the Carlingford peninsula in the far northeast, and back.

Much of the action takes place on the border of ancient Ulster, still wholly recognisable today. The modern road to Belfast runs past the selfsame Gap of the North defended by Cuchulainn against Queen Medb. The border today replicates the ancient one. Those who think that Ireland's

⌗ *Co. Roscommon*

The great journey of Táin Bó Cuailnge begins in Co. Roscommon and erupts eastward across the River Shannon. I have an inborn tendency to see this as the trajectory of human existence, since I too originated there and was projected eastwards. The brazen clamour of the Cattle-Raid of Cooley had dwindled to an anecdote in the country of my childhood. People were tired of being thatched and patched and backward; we wanted to be modern but did not know how. The bungalow, the picture-window, the TV set had not yet arrived.

My parents were primary-school teachers and we kept a few cows near Athleague, a quiet village where nothing much had happened since Red Hugh O'Donnell crossed the River Suck in 1601 on his march to Kinsale.

It was my job to feed the calves and milk the cows by hand in the evenings after school. Sadly there was no cattle-raiding to be had, though I remember Fair Days in Roscommon town, rain teeming down, the windows barricaded, and steaming beasts packed together up and down the streets in a stew of dung. Cattle-dealers stamped about in boots, with heavy sticks, grunting take-it-or-leave-it prices that were only a hair's-breadth from theft-with-menace.

I treated cows as the enormous lumbering pets they are, and walked them home for milking with my arms slung across a pair of rolling necks behind the stumpy horns, feet lifted pleasantly off the ground between them. A red shorthorn made her way home from miles away, days after she had been sold.

The black cat watched the milking from the cowshed door. The trick was to build up a head of pressure in the udder, working fast with two hands, then squirt the cat full in the chest across the floor. She was caught between outrage and gratitude; forever feeling towards a scheme to attract the milk without the drenching – a great lesson in evolution for both of us. Ringworm was the result of all this handling, with visits to the seventh son of a seventh son, near Athleague, for a cure.

divisions began with British interference might read Táin Bó Cuailnge carefully and reach the conclusion that the split may be as old as history itself. It is a fracture in the mould.

 # Royal Squabble

There is a soap-opera scene at the start of Táin Bó Cuailnge. It's a curtain-raiser in which egos are inflamed and the journey towards battle, bloodshed and betrayal is set in motion. Queen Medb and her royal consort, Ailill, lying in bed in Cruachain, engage in a clash of connubial pride. The charged pillow-talk of a king and queen, nearly two thousand years ago, triggers the journey from Connacht to Ulster to capture the brown bull of Cooley. The tone of post-coital rancour is familiar to us from television-drama, where no one has the sense to shut up in bed.

'It's well for the wife of a wealthy man,' King Ailill blusters. 'You're much better off today than the day I married you.'

'I was well enough off without you,' Queen Medb retorts. And that should have been warning enough.

Medb reminds Ailill that her father, the High King of Ireland, bestowed the province of Connacht on her. She has a tidy way of putting it in Thomas Kinsella's translation: 'You're a kept man!'

And so the epic comparison of wealth begins – the pairing of beast and herd and species, bringing to mind Noah's preparations and the probability that a common narrative flourish underpins all such tales of ancient accountancy. In the heel of the reel, Ailill owns a magnificent white bull, *Finnbennach*, for which Medb has no match. The crooked corner of some narrator's mouth hisses that Finnbennach was the calf of one of Queen Medb's cows; he went over to the king's herd, refusing to be led by a woman. And so begins Medb's savage journey northeastward to Ulster, to rob a matching bull from Carlingford and to cut her husband down to size.

But the underlying thrust of the story, and of the journey, runs far deeper than a domestic squabble. It is an account of the conflict between the early provinces and tribes of Ireland – the ebb and flow of power that would shape the country for centuries to come.

Rathcroghan

Covering an area of about four square miles on a plateau northwest of Tulsk in Co. Roscommon, the royal site of *Cruachain*, or Rathcroghan, is one of the great ritual landscapes of Ireland, in a league that includes the Boyne Valley, *Emain Macha* (Navan Fort) and Tara. In spite of such breathless significance, there is not a whole lot to see. Some fifty scattered mounds and earthworks – Rathmore, Rathbeg, Rathnadarve – are printed on a careless landscape, which is little more than rumpled by their presence. They look, on a huge scale, like a set of casual objects covered by a rug moulded to their shapes by rain.

Round about, the usual fenced and stonewalled fields enclose the unkempt architecture of rural Ireland. Within their shelter-belts of sycamore, conifer and whitethorn, the houses are up to their knees in the past. Only a grassy sward separates them from the subsoil of history. The twisting N5, between Tulsk and Frenchpark, is a smear of tarmac across an ancient plain.

Left: Glenreemore, Co. Wicklow. Art O'Neill is believed to have died here, January 1592, while escaping with Red Hugh O'Donnell from Dublin Castle.

Right: The restored O'Donnell Castle, Donegal town.

Left: MacClancy's castle on Lough Melvin, defended by Captain de Cuéllar, with eight Spanish soldiers against an army of seventeen hundred.

Below: On the shore of Lough Melvin, Co. Leitrim, opposite MacClancy's Castle.

Above: Benbulben from Streedagh Strand, where Captain Francisco de Cuéllar came ashore, September 1588.

Below: Benbulben, Co. Sligo.

Above: Hidden valley near Glengarriff on the Beara Peninsula, Co. Cork.

Opposite top left: Carriganass Castle, Co. Cork, New Year's Eve, 2002. Re-enactment of O'Sullivan's March.

Opposite top right: Entrance to *Uaimh na gCat* at Cruachain (Rathcroghan), Co. Roscommon. Lair of the Morrígan, goddess of war in the Táin. (Note the fetishes on the bush).

Opposite bottom: *Lios an tSeagail*, a ringfort in the Cooley Mountains, Co. Louth. The great Brown Bull of Cooley was hidden here, in the Táin.

Below: Ruins of Dunboy Castle, home of O'Sullivan Beare, Co. Cork.

Above: Gaelic Apache in the Curlew Mountains, Sligo/Roscommon.

Below: River Shannon, at Clonmacnoise, Co. Offaly. Scene of a ninth-century bridge to Connacht.

Above: Layered landscape on Brian Boru's route. Many early features are still visible.

Below: Winter sunrise in Wicklow.

Above: St Patrick at Ogulla, near Tulsk, Co. Roscommon.

Below: The author in the Burren, Co. Clare.

There is a car park, a landscaped bank with planted shrubs and wand-like rowans wavering in the wind. Midday, in mid-June, there is no one here. 'Rathcroghan', the display on stout galvanised poles proclaims: 'Royal Residence'.

In its earliest visible phase, this was a prehistoric cemetery, belonging to a people of whose language we know nothing. Recent inhabitants (our Celtic ancestors) named it from *cruacha*, the Irish for 'mounds'. They imagined palaces and royal halls here, just as they did at Tara farther to the east. So they centred their own kingdom of Connacht on this location, locking their transient structures into a powerful landscape for enhanced authority. *Cruachain* is thought to have become a place of ritual assembly for the inauguration of provincial kings. It was never a hub of palaces and banqueting halls as it is often visualised, out in the wilds like Las Vegas.

Still, whatever way you look at it, there is not a lot to see – apart from dawn and sunset and weather and cattle. But, with *second* sight, which is not so difficult to acquire, a place like this has so much resonance that it practically hums under human scrutiny. The hum is in the observer's head, of course. It is the consensus of time. The place has been felt with such intensity for thousands of years; so much curiosity has accumulated that there is a current of concentration charging the air – or rather the space within the observer's head. The speculation of countless generations, ever aware of significance, aligns our thoughts like iron filings in a magnetic current.

෨ *Gates of Hell*

The trapdoor of the Underworld is actually located in *Cruachain*. Savage beasts, pagan devils, forces bent on wreaking havoc broke through to terrorise the upper world. When I was growing up, people kept quiet about such things. Bad enough to be known as Roscommon Sheep-stealers; unforgivable to have the Gates of Hell in the county.

Uaimh na gCat, Cave of the Cats, is marked on a map of the monuments about half a mile southwest of Rathcroghan Mound. A wood-sculptor living nearby led me to the end of a narrow road, under a sycamore tree. He pointed out a pit like a badger sett among the roots of a heavy whitethorn. The branches were snagged with fetishes of ribbon and rag, such as you find at a holy well.

A section of the cave is accessible by crawling under the bush, through the constricted opening, and down a muddy shaft. Ireland is riddled with limestone caves that would swallow this one without trace, but the chamber, for all its slimy constriction, is striking. Its eeriness is a result of the intensity of tradition and the stories associated with it. Crawling in, I felt as though I was entering a crack in the floor of time. There is another crack in the floor of the imagination that coincides with it during a visit and allows the past to break through into the mind

Just over one hundred feet long, twenty feet high at the most, the narrow channel dips to a muddy floor between dripping walls, the ground rising steeply at the far end, and the sides closing in to form a bottleneck blocked by excavation damage from above. Wedged in a greasy slot, almost out of reach, was a hard black object, twice the size of my hand. When I wiped away the muck, the torchlight revealed a three-faced head of astonishing sharpness and clarity. I thought of the evil figure known as the Morrígan, one of three manifestations of the goddess of war. Her name derives from *MórRíoghain*, the Great Queen. This triple-personage of the ancient world (our gods still come in threes) is known to have dwelt for a time in the cave at *Cruachain*. She harried the Táin on its journey east, appearing in various guises, from a beautiful girl to a powerful eel, a grey she-wolf, a hornless red heifer …. There she was, in the torchlight, at the end of the cave, black as an ember of hell. I found out later that Davy, the wood-sculptor, had placed her there in a personal handshake with the past.

THE MEN OF IRELAND

Led by Medb and Ailill, the army left Rathcroghan and marched towards the River Shannon. The great cattle-raid to capture the brown bull of Cooley was under way. They camped the first night at *Cuil Silinne*, Kilcooley, just east of Tulsk today. There is a country graveyard there, overlooking the main road. A few tall yew trees transcend the ordinariness at twilight and lend it an air of belonging to a different time. The army in that encampment numbered fifty-four thousand. It was made up of eighteen troops, each of three thousand men. They were allies from every corner of the country, including a detachment of exiled Ulstermen under Fergus mac Róich, who was Queen Medb's lover.[1]

Inspecting her troops at Kilcooley, Medb observed that the *Gaileoin*, Leinstermen, excelled all the other groups in every skill. They had their shelters pitched, their food eaten, their musicians tuned up, while the rest were still preparing to cook. Medb warned her husband and her lover that these Gaileoin would reap all the glory of the war if they were allowed to continue. But she would not have them left behind, for fear they would capture her territory in revenge. Ailill and Fergus were openly impatient. What would she have them do with the Gaileoin?

'Kill them!' she commanded.

'That's a woman's thinking and no mistake,' Ailill scorned.

Fergus swore that the Gaileoin would be killed over his dead body. Medb did not flinch. 'That can be arranged.'

❧ Queen Medb of Connacht

Who was this virago? Did she ever exist, or is she a grotesque spasm of the ancestral imagination?

In the Táin, Medb is queen of the Connachtmen, her territory centred on *Cruachain*. However, she actually originated as the goddess of sovereignty at Tara in the eastern province of Leinster. She is known to have been the focus through which a pagan king was married to his land. Medb – meaning roughly 'one who intoxicates' – was invoked by alcohol during the inauguration ritual of a king. The alcohol was fermented honey, known as mead.

The Connachta were originally an elite based at Tara in Leinster. From that power-base, they harried the northern province of Ulster in the early centuries of the first millennium AD. They split into tribes east and west of the Shannon while the Táin tales were developing. Connachta, the original name of the tribe, became the province of Connacht, where some of the group remained, while others continued to dominate Tara as the Uí Néill.

As the Táin stories developed to keep pace with political change, Medb was shifted to *Cruachain*, royal centre of the Connachta or Connachtmen, and she was transmuted to a common queen. At some stage in this transformation, the memory of her matings with many kings gave her a sexual dimension that would guarantee her popularity in the Christian imagination. Along with every deal struck throughout the Táin, she offers a bonus: '... and the friendship of my thighs on top of that.'

Fergus mac Róich, chief incumbent of those thighs, bitterly turned the position around, when he pronounced after the final battle, 'We followed the rump of a misguiding woman. It is the usual thing for a herd led by a mare to be strayed and destroyed.'

It is quite clear that the Táin has a sustained misogynistic slant, which must reflect both the warrior culture from which it emerged and the monastic culture that wrote it down. It reflects also the inhuman divinity from which Queen Medb was drawn.

 RIVER SHANNON

Soon after the army left *Cruachain*, the River Shannon barred the way. No fuss was made of the crossing, but it would have been a major challenge. The river was wider then. Animals and loads had to be brought across. There were high spots and dry spots at a ford; there were shoals and shallows and makeshift causeways. Fords depended on slack water, which meant that travel and raiding were seasonal. It must have been a disaster to be caught by floods in enemy terrain on the wrong side of a river.

There were several options and Medb's army used the ford closest to Rathcroghan.[2] The Táin force of fifty-four thousand warriors crossed at the point where the linear village of Tarmonbarry now stands on the western bank and the Longford-bound N5 bridges the Shannon. The exemplary Gaileoin warriors had been scattered among the other troops.

If the Táin had originated as a story of Connacht attacking Ulster, the army would probably have crossed at the Doon of Drumsna further upriver, and headed directly north. The choice of the Carlingford Peninsula in the far northeast as a destination suits a campaign beginning in Tara, as this one probably did in some earlier, oral version

On the trail of the Táin, I found it an anticlimax to cross the Shannon at Tarmonbarry. The road-bridge seemed to miss the point. There is a very powerful weir just a few hundred feet downstream. A railed gangway suspended over the flood crosses the river at this point, closed off at either end. It is guarded during the day, but I dodged across at dawn before the sentry mounted the rampart with his bugle and spear. Mist and spray were rising off the roiling river. Pent-up waters roared in the channels under the quivering gangway. Staring down into the thunder where the water was squeezed into jets of liquid marble, I understood for the first time the strength of this river which had always seemed asleep in its wandering flow. Clenching the rail with whitened knuckles, I felt the gangway thrust back upstream against the surge, as if I stood at the rail of an ocean-going ship.

We don't feel this elemental sense of power while crossing any bridge today. We have forgotten that the Shannon was once the main travel route in Ireland. Our lives are rarely engaged with the river now, except as recreation; we don't depend on the surrounding land for food or security. A bridge today is part of that detachment, a means of soaring across a current without even glancing aside.

And yet, when bridges were first constructed, they must have seemed a miracle: timber and stone suspended in air, challenging the force of the flood. They collapsed and were swept away, were thrown down by defenders and invaders time and again, reinforcing the dominance of the river, which for all the security it offered was also fraught with the threat of attack.

The Vikings sailed up the Shannon on frequent raids. Brian Boru put three hundred boats on the river as part of his bid for the kingship of Ireland. Barricades of stone were constructed across the river to deter him. Warring expeditions on the Shannon are known to have portaged their boats overland to join other river systems. In 1139, the King of Connacht held a muster during which a canal was dug between the Suck and the Shannon. So great was the threat of Napoleonic invasion via the Shannon that powerful defences were constructed as far upriver as Meelick.

Despite all that, and numerous wicker-bridges at Athlone, Connacht can be seen as an almost-island on any map that gives due prominence to the Shannon. From the gaping fissure of the estuary, the river is a severe crack-line that runs most of the way around the province towards Sligo Bay. A province is only a territorial state of mind floating on the land, but in the case of Connacht, the Shannon is a definitive boundary. Given the kind of labour that built *Cruachain* and fortified the Doon of Drumsna, it should not have been all that hard to apply primitive leverage and snap Connacht off decisively, making it an island for practical purposes. Archimedes, in the same period, spoke of a lever long enough to shift a planet.

When I was growing up in Roscommon, the bridges on the Shannon were fixed in the psyche of the Connachtman like crossings into another state of mind. Chugging east through Athlone, over the narrow bridge in a boxy Ford, there was a sense of reaching a foreign shore. That feeling has not completely vanished, even with the opening of the new bridge that bypassed Athlone. But, as we swoop across the broad current of the river now, we no longer feel we are entering treacherous Leinster and the shadow of Britain. Given the circle of stars and the funding acknowledgements, there is little doubt that we have reached Europe.

 # Co. Longford

East of the Shannon, Medb's army entered *Trego*, the Plain of the Spears, flat ground stretching a few short miles to Longford town.

There was no sense of political unity in Ireland in the pagan Iron Age, although shifting alliances existed. The political and social unit was the *tuath*, the local king's domain. These were petty kings of little substance, ruling scattered tribes. Only within his own *tuath*, under the protection of his own leader, did a person have an identity and security. The intellectual classes and the craftsmen, the *aes dána*, were the exceptions. They seem to have travelled widely and to have been responsible eventually for the unified culture of a fractured country.

 # WARRIORS

The appearance of the Iron Age raiding-band would have been very different from that depicted in the Táin, which is bursting with well-armed heroes in chariots, all coiffed, cloaked and bejewelled.[3] Colour was added as the story developed over many centuries from the pagan Iron Age into the Christian era when versions of it were finally written down. The actual warriors would have been a straggling mass of tribesmen, dressed in motley wool and rawhide, ill-disciplined and crudely armed. Disfigurement and physical handicap would have been rife. An expert eye would have recognised different groups by hair colour and bone structure, relating them to their area of origin, as one might even today at a football final, or at the fair at Ballinasloe. Many were of the longstanding genetic stock of the island with no Celtic identity, apart from the new Gaelic language that was erasing the earlier tongues.

While the Táin paints them all as heroes, some groups must have reeked of misery, while others were aggressive, or raucous and jovial. There were long-boned men in family groups; short men with stubby legs and potbellies; there were thick necks and scrawny Adam's apples; curly-headed easygoing men, famous perhaps for the beauty of their women, and jealous types who lost their tempers in a flash and were easily killed in battle. Some would be friendly by nature, others permanently suspicious, sensing a slight in everything. Each group had its own leader. The promise of plunder and loot would have kept them all together.

Bigger groups had in train their women, cooks, porters and healers. Professional warriors had their own attendants. The chariot was a feature of the European Celts that filtered into Ireland along with a number of military practices. Although chariots were popular in the legends, it is doubtful that they were common on a rugged journey with many fords to be crossed. Provisions were carried on horseback – also by porters and slaves. There would not have been enough food for a long journey, so stops had to be scheduled for hunting and raiding along the way. People living beside the route in settlements of thatched huts would have fled with their stock at the first hint of a war party approaching. Or else, deals might be done, either by force or negotiation, to supply food for the march. Local groups joining Medb's army in Longford and further east must have pitched in a beast or two, or a sack of corn, in exchange for a promise of plunder. The brown bull of Cooley is an elite symbol. In real life, the Men of Ireland were raiding Ulster for cattle, for women and for slaves.

✳ GRANARD

At this point, the Táin army was conscious of being observed – an uneasy feeling in the back of the neck. A prophecy of doom was bayed aloud in the camp at Longford, and the war spirit left the troops terrified and sleepless. Groups started up in panic, prepared to flee for home, no doubt, until Medb came and calmed them. Next day, the army headed for high ground – not easy to find, it might be thought, in the central plain of Ireland, dented as it is by the weight of an ice age. But, in fact, the plain is studded with ridges. The town of Granard lifts to a central hill with huge views across the countryside in all directions. There are hills sketched in the distance on every horizon. Enemies moving out there would have been visible to Medb's army from their camp at Granard.

Fergus, the Ulster exile, chief tactician of Medb's army, sent a message north to his former comrades, warning of Medb's attack – a delicate exercise in loyalty and betrayal. He knew that the Ulster army, to a man, was flat on its back. The northern warriors suffered the pangs of childbirth in times of emergency. This was the vengeance of Macha, another aspect of the war goddess, who had cursed the Ulstermen for forcing her to race the king's chariot while she was pregnant.[4]

Granard is dominated by a tall church, Gothic Revival, with a darkly elegant spire. A grassy dome peers oddly over the shoulder of the church. It is a prominent Norman 'motte', heaped up on the highest point of the landscape. Long before any church was built, this flat-topped mound had a timber stockade around the perimeter of the summit, enclosing a wooden tower. No doubt it incorporated earlier fortifications on this strategic position, and probably prehistoric structures as well. Medb's army would have posted lookouts there, perhaps a thousand years before the Normans came in the twelfth century.

Today, a statue of St Patrick dominates the mound. It commemorates fifteen hundred years of Irish Christianity. The broken hand and the rusty claw, typical of ageing statues, suggest the iron will required to convert a pagan country and to throw that steep spire skywards within a shout of the ancient mound.

The army of the Táin was about to come under the surveillance of Cuchulainn, the Hound of Ulster. Well might their neck hairs bristle. Born on the Plain of Muirtheimhne, east of Dundalk, he was exempt from the phantom pregnancy that crippled the northern warriors. The defence of the province fell to him.

Cuchulainn's qualities in the Táin have a definite sense of plurality about them. His hair is of three distinct kinds – 'brown at the base, blood red in the middle, with a crown of golden yellow'. He has seven irises in each eye, seven fingers on each hand. The sheer force of his role would justify its division among a sizeable crowd.

Cuchulainn observed the Táin journey first from the hill of *Iraird Cuillenn*, which is Crossakeel in Co. Meath – high ground, though not quite in the moral sense, because he abandoned his post to spend the night with a slave-girl provided for his use.

∾ *Cuchulainn*

There is evidence that Cuchulainn was freshly inserted into the Táin on a cut-and-paste basis, as the version we are familiar with took shape. His character and role are complete, but they developed in some other narrative context and were trimmed to fit the Táin. An earlier text exists, with a synopsis of the Táin in which Cuchulainn is not mentioned at all. His role is played by Fiacc, a son of Fergus mac Róich.

However, the end result is an idealised warrior with the ultimate skills. He carries echoes of the continental Celts described by Roman writers, and it seems likely that his lore grew from an early Celtic war-cult settled somewhere near Dundalk in the late Iron Age.

The role of this group may have been the frontline defence of Ulster. Such a warrior tribe, perhaps with experience against the Romans in Europe, would have been logical allies of the Ulaidh (the Ulstermen) reacting against Uí Néill (Connachta) expansionism from Tara. That such an expansion did occur historically is beyond doubt, and Ulster shrank dramatically as a result. Gradually the war band came to be embodied in a single figure. The fact that the early Irish practised single combat must have added to the cult of the warrior as hero, and furthermore the prospect of a fight to the death between two rival characters, Ferdia and Cuchulainn (echoed later in the battle of the two bulls) had the dramatic potential to turn the Táin from a complex war campaign into a personal struggle of epic proportions.

As he whittles away at Medb's army, paring it down, it becomes logical to think of Cuchulainn historically as a band of guerrillas harrying an army in wild terrain. That tactic would distinguish Gaelic warfare against superior forces many centuries later.

MIDLAND CHARM

Medb's army quit the heights of Granard and headed for Crossakeel, where Cuchulainn had stood to observe them. Today, the pursuit of the Táin through this landscape south of Lough Sheelin provides one of the most unexpectedly rewarding road journeys in Ireland. This is thoroughly midland country, where the topography could be expected to be as flat as the accent. In fact, it is a thicket of tangled landscape with twisting back-roads in a tumble of hills; nothing high, but none of it flat; everything smothered in hedges and native trees. There is a casual richness and, above all, a relaxation to the countryside that seems to have retained tradition and resisted intensive change. The absence of Sitka spruce is striking.

Somewhere outside Granard, there is a dancehall from the mid-twentieth century that catches the eye as forcefully as a prehistoric ruin. The degree of decay in a few short decades is shocking. Some of those who danced to the showbands are living out along the roads to Finea. The stark new houses common to the midlands are rare in this area, but there is a scatter of older farmhouses and cottages with slate roofs, limestone walls, stone gateposts, iron gates. Now and then, a hood of ivy on some ancient gable appears, or a country rose growing up a whitewashed wall. A little black-haired girl stands at a gate, with a calendar-kitten in her arms, a dog peering over the wall. Another child, a few miles further on, in a sleeveless T-shirt, has a tattoo on her shoulder, where the rim of a different culture has broken through. Fat cattle lie low in the afternoon, stupefied with grass. Four brown ponies graze among buttercups in a field surrounded by drumlins. There are no – almost no – dormer bungalows with tight black caps of imitation slate and those plastic doors with the crimped expression – the type that give off toxic fumes in a house fire.

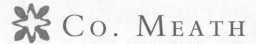

Co. Meath

Crossakeel stands at a height of one hundred and sixty metres. The unpretentious village has a big sky and a wide view. Gently accessible, it is the ideal vantage point from which to survey terrain that would be quite hidden at a lower elevation. This is Ireland from a defensive perspective, an Iron Age point of view. A forecast of doom for the Men of Ireland at the bloody hands of Cuchulainn was issued here. The seer warned of 'torn corpses, women wailing', and chanted in a complex Gaelic metre:

> *Whole hosts he will destroy,*
> *Making dense massacre.*
> *In thousands you will yield your heads …*

Crossakeel draws no attention to its role in prehistory. But there is an echo of the ancient poet's warning in a verse from 'The Red Flag' on a brand-new monument. The labour anthem was written by a local man:

> *The people's Flag is deepest red;*
> *It shrouded oft our martyred dead*
> *And ere their limbs grew stiff or cold,*
> *Their hearts' blood dyed its ev'ry fold …*

Seen from an Iron Age perspective, the most potent feature in this landscape is *Sliabh na Cailli* (Hag's mountain) crowned by Lough Crew megalithic cemetery just a few miles away to the northwest. This low ridge of limestone hills has been described as 'a virtual necropolis'. Dozens of tombs in various stages of exposure dot the hilltops, some clearly visible from Crossakeel. Dating from roughly 3000 BC, the passage-grave cemetery has a sense of casual access that makes it in ways more attractive than the highly managed Boyne Valley tombs of roughly the same period.

Sliabh Caillí offers historic views, mythic perspectives. Those would have been the summer uplands of a cattle culture, and highlands too of the imagination. The ridge provides a hill-walk among clusters of passage graves in a part of Ireland where the average walker would swear that no hill exists.

For the early Irish, including those travelling with the Táin, the passage graves and cairns were the homes of Otherworld communities living within the earth. These mounds were called *sidhe* and this word gradually came to be attributed to the beings who dwelt in them. The lore was transmuted into the later cult of the fairies, or the *Sí*.

As the Táin army pondered its route at Crossakeel and opted for a detour south to avoid Cuchulainn, the warriors were probably looking over the tops of trees at the tombs of Lough Crew rising above native forest. The rich lands around Crossakeel were farmed sporadically from the Neolithic Age onwards, beginning five to six thousand years ago. During the centuries to which the Táin belongs, there was a dramatic decline in Iron Age agriculture. Wild woodland prevailed for several hundred years, until roughly the beginning of Christianity. This was a dark period, possibly of strife and population decline, accompanied by phases of poor weather. It is not difficult to imagine famine, plague and campaigns of war.

An early Irish army would have followed well-trodden general routes. There was an axe-wielding engineer corps to facilitate sudden detours. The charioteers, and there cannot have been many, were skilled in tackling obstacles. A small amount of seasoned timber would be carried for running repairs. Ash must have been particularly useful where lightness, flexibility and strength were required. Although only the wheel appears in early carvings, some version of the slide-car seems more likely for ease of passage over wet ground and unavoidable areas of bog. The horses were small and light, a trend that was to continue in the military exploitation of Ireland. When an army moved under pressure, as in the retreat at the end of the Táin, a trail of debris and baggage would have been left behind.

 # Taboo

Cuchulainn imposed a ritual prohibition on the progress of Medb's army. His *geis*, or taboo, was carved in Ogham script on a wooden peg, inscribed with one hand only, an echo of some ancient magical practice, a druidic ritual perhaps. The *geis* in heroic tales often reads as a kind of tedious mannerism, disrupting the narrative logic. But it suited a cultural mindset where superstition and belief in the forces of the Otherworld were powerful influences.

Rather than challenge Cuchulainn, the army made a detour to the south, and the trees were hacked down before the chariots. The diversion was known as *Slechta*, the hewn place. This is a self-evident image of how roads came into being. It took them south towards the present Kilsceer and east to *Ceanannas*, or Kells. This historic little town has always

struggled with its identity. (Ceanannas means 'great residence' while Kells means 'churches'.) It used to be called
Cuil Sibrille as well. It was to be known as Kenlis, an Anglo-
Norman corruption of Ceanannas, before it became Kells;
then it reverted to Ceanannas, which seems not to have
caught on, because it is still widely known as Kells.

During the night, a great snow fell on the Connacht army
camped at Ceanannas. It reached 'over the men's belts and
the chariot wheels'. This was unseasonable, to say the least,
as they were hardly travelling in winter. The snow was a narrative flourish, provided by some thoughtful storyteller, and
it was dismissed afterwards by a sudden thaw. Having spent
the night with a woman, in dereliction of his sentry duty,
Cuchulainn was tracking Medb's army. Cuchulainn's skill
was immense but the count confused him, until he guessed
that one troop of three thousand had been dispersed among
fifty thousand soldiers. These were the Gaileoin of course,
broken up and scattered on Medb's orders before crossing
the Shannon.

Coincidentally, when St Patrick was on the nearby Hill of
Tara, launching Christianity in the late Iron Age, he got into
a contest of miracles with a druid who covered the countryside with snow for openers. St Patrick removed it in response. Maybe this was the same snowfall and thaw that
took the Táin by surprise, dating the journey a little later
than was thought – to the fifth century!

 ATTACK

The journey continued past the Hill of Slane and veered
northeast of the Bend of the Boyne. This brought the army

onto the route of *Slí Mhidluachra* (one of the so-called Five Great Roads) heading northwards from Tara to *Emain Macha*, royal centre of Ulster. This ancient route crossed the Boyne at the famous Ford of the Brow just below Newgrange. A few miles further north, it forded the River Mattock, close to the point where Medb's army joined the route. It was at *Ath Gabhla*, Ford of the Fork on the Mattock, that Cuchulainn first attacked Medb's warriors, killing four of the finest, who were travelling in front, 'keeping their rugs and cloaks and brooches from being soiled by the dusts of the multitude'. For all their pains, their garments and their gear were soiled in gore and their heads impaled on a forked tree-trunk, thrust into the bed of the ford. Too late to turn back then ...

This is one of the most densely historic areas in Ireland, with a number of symbolic sites within reach, each marking the climax of an era, or a major turning point. Just behind, to the south, the Bend in the Boyne itself was created as recently as twelve thousand years ago, as the glaciers of the last Ice Age retreated. The glacial soil left in the new loop of the river allowed the development of a Neolithic culture rich enough to construct the megalithic tombs, Newgrange, Knowth and Dowth, five thousand years ago.

What did the Iron Age warriors think as they ploughed their way through the landscape of the Boyne? It's a good bet that the Connachtmen were grumbling about the quality of their own land compared to these verdant plains of *Midhe*. Thoughts of their bony cattle on the sour grass of home must have sharpened their taste for the pillaging and raiding not too far ahead. In time, as they expanded, the Connachta would take over these lands and push the Laigin/Leinstermen southwards out of *Midhe*.

Early in the first millennium AD, the Roman Andalusian, Pomponius Mela, wrote of Ireland: '… the weather does not suit the ripening of grain, but there is plenty of grass that is juicy and even sweet; with the result that the cattle are full after part of the day, and if they were not kept from eating they would burst.' He added, 'The people are uncivilised; more ignorant of virtue than other nations ….' This was sour grapes, of course, as the belief that the grain necessary to feed an army could not be grown here was partly responsible for keeping the Romans out.

The sequence of Christian sites on the Táin journey demonstrates the monastic eye for good land close to a major route. Today, the impact of the ruins depends on the approach. The broken tower of Monasterboice seen from the N1 motorway at 70 mph is not an arresting sight. It arouses a transient curiosity, a sense that it might be nice to visit sometime, but not now. However, if Monasterboice is approached by the oldest local road, travelling north from Drogheda on the Táin-route called *Belach nAne* ('the way they drove'), the tower thrusts powerfully through a canopy of trees and looks like a volcanic plug from which the ground has fallen away. The real treasures in the enclosure are the huge stone crosses, silently revealing the confidence of their makers, and dwarfing the modern imitations. But there was no trace of Christian building in the landscape as the hordes of the Táin moved north.

SLINGSHOT

Beyond the fringes of the march, Cuchulainn met a Connacht charioteer cutting wood for repairs. Thinking he was one of Medb's men, the driver asked him to trim the holly-shafts he had cut. The young warrior pulled a thick pole through his fist, stripping off the knots and bark, and paring the shaft clean. The Connachtman was terrified but Cuchulainn reassured him that he had no quarrel with drivers.

The broken chariot belonged to a son of Medb and Ailill, who was waiting nearby. Cuchulainn lopped the prince's head off, placed it on the charioteer's back, and told him to bring it to Medb and Ailill in that exact position. Otherwise he too would lose his head.

The charioteer ran up to Medb and Ailill with the news. In his fright, he lifted their son's head from his back. Immediately, a stone from a slingshot shattered his skull.

'It is not true therefore,' the tale declares, 'that Cuchulainn did not kill charioteers; he killed them if they did wrong.'

Many more heads were lost to Cuchulainn's skill before a strange little event occurred to pinpoint the army's position on the east coast at the mouth of the River Fane, just south of Blackrock village and Dundalk.

With a slingshot, Cuchulainn knocked a pet bird and a squirrel off Medb's shoulders. Two ancient place names arising from the incident refer to twin shoulders of land at the mouth of the River Fane. They are *Méthe Tog*, Squirrel Neck and *Méthe nEuin*, Bird Neck. (*Tog* is more accurately translated as a pine marten. The ancient word *méthe*, meaning a headless stump, can still be found in a modern Irish dictionary.)

The story demonstrates in the first place that the army was on the correct route for the fording of Dundalk Bay; further, it shows how intricately oral narrative is bound into naming the landscape, and how difficult it can be to tell which came first – the place name, or its story.

The Táin is obsessive in this practice. Plot and action are often subservient to place, or the naming of it. It reflects a powerful mechanism in early Gaelic culture which is formalised in the bardic art of *Dinnseanchas*, the lore of place. This focus has influenced Irish literature ever since, so that it should be no surprise at all that *Ulysses*, the ultimate novel of place, is located in the Irish consciousness.

DUNDALK BAY

They had left the Great North Road, *Slí Mhidluachra*, by then and were following a course that would take them across Dundalk Bay at low tide, and deep into the Cooley Peninsula. This shortcut might save a day over the long way round, which crossed the Castletown River at a ford in present-day Dundalk, passing dangerously close to Cuchulainn's home. Apparently it was still possible to cross the Bay to Rockmarshall on the Cooley Peninsula until the central channel was dredged in 1905. But even the most credulous traveller would find it hard to visualise an army – chariots, supply train and camp followers – crossing the sludge of the bay at any time. The mud is odiously glutinous. That route could have been taken by an advance force of muck-savages working a pincer-movement while the main army kept to the west of Dundalk.

COOLEY MOUNTAINS

Having invaded Cooley in spite of Cuchulainn, or the border tribe he represented, Medb's army set up headquarters at Finnabair Cuailnge, a big rath not far from the place now

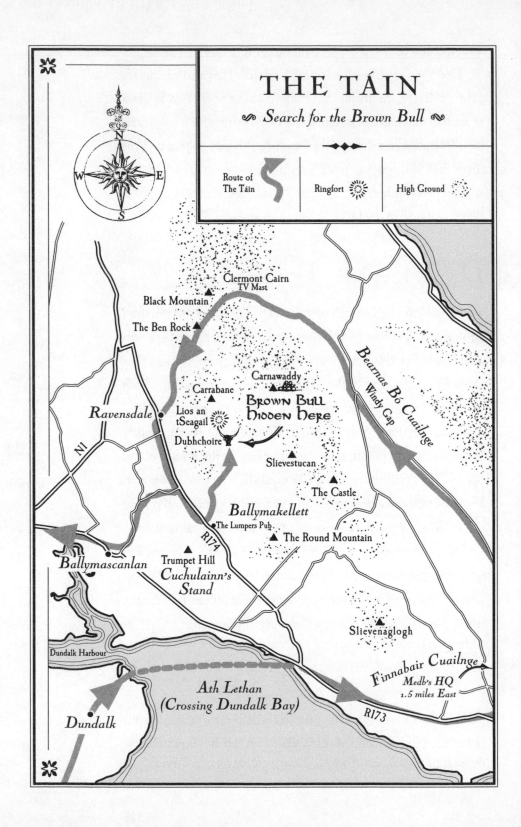

called 'The Bush', a former railway station on the Carlingford road. Densely overgrown, this rath, flanked by a local water-scheme, is still a significant feature in the landscape. Seen through briars, nettles and blackthorn, a high mound is visible within. It has a flattened top, suggesting a Norman 'motte' rather than a ringfort.

The invaders were running out of time, the recovery of the ailing Ulstermen imminent. The army split up in search of *Donn Cuailnge*, the brown bull of Cooley. They ravaged the surrounding countryside. Medb took her troops on a blood-thirsty mission out of Cooley and deeper into Ulster, bent on destruction. Her route carved northwards through the Cooley Mountains and out onto the Midluachair road again. She is credited with having gouged out the 'The Windy Gap', or *Bearnas Bó Cuailnge*, as a deliberate insult to the men of Ulster.

But it was not Medb who levelled the even older court tomb in the Windy Gap. That ancient monument was destroyed by the modern widening of the road. It has picked up an accretion of folklore to become 'The Long Woman's Grave'.

Medb's journey further north refused to take the simple lowland route along the Newry river to join *Slí Mhidluachra*. Floods on the mountain rivers forced the army upwards over the ridge of Black Mountain at almost five hundred metres, and down the western slopes to the Flurry River and Ravensdale, the area called *Bélat Ailiúin* in the Táin. And indeed there are extravagant river gorges in this part of the Cooleys, quite out of proportion to the little streams they now contain. It is understandable that such a landscape inspired the flood reports that saturate these episodes of the Táin.

Medb's route is actually a very pleasant traverse of the secondary ridge of the Cooleys (Slieve Foye being the primary). Various routes lead to the prominent cairn known as Carnawaddy, and then the broad ridge is followed in a northerly direction towards the TV mast on Black Mountain. An ancient track, a green road, leads down the hillside, heading south towards Ravensdale. *An Poc Fada*, an annual hurling competition, is held on these slopes. The winner is the one who traverses the mountain with the lowest number of strokes. Carnawaddy (Cairn of the Dog), where the hurlers begin their descent, is reputed to be the burial mound of Fionn Mac Cumhail's hound, Bran. It is certainly some kind of burial chamber, but its exact nature is uncertain. Clermont Cairn, to the north along the ridge, is a megalithic passage tomb.

This is the area in which the brown bull was concealed by the Ulstermen. *Dubhchoire*, the Black Cauldron, is a deceptive little valley, hidden from sight in a fold of the hills to the west of Ravensdale. Without a map, or prior knowledge, it would be difficult to spot the tiny, glaciated valley from the main Dublin–Belfast road, no more than three miles away. A ridge of rounded hills, Doolargy and Carrabane, blends into the higher, heathery slopes behind, crowned by Carnawaddy. *Dubhchoire* is hidden in full sight.

The little valley is best approached from the townland of Ballymakellett, in the vicinity of the 'Lumpers' pub, on the R174 between Jenkinstown and Ravensdale. Minor roads and lanes lead upwards into the folded hills. These slopes are known in the Táin as Glenn Gat, the Valley of the Osiers. The Ordnance Survey map and the Archaeological Survey of Co. Louth reveal an area liberally speckled with monuments.

HIDEAWAY

The most striking feature is the ringfort known as Lissa-chiggle (*Lios an tSeagail* – Fort of the Rye) on the 250-metre contour at the back of the little corrie formed by Doolargy and Carrabane. Hidden, yet accessible, plentifully supplied with water, *Lios an tSeagail* seems an ideal hiding place for a valuable animal. It is, however, clearly visible to anyone on the slopes immediately above. There is a more secure place of concealment a couple of miles to the southeast, in the extraordinary ravine that runs steeply down to Ballymakellett from an opening between Slievestucan and the Castle. This is a far more likely source of the willows that would have given rise to the name *Glenn Gat*, Valley of the Osiers, in which the black cauldron was located.

However, the stone-built ringfort, *Lios an tSeagail*, holds a more romantic appeal. To the east, a short slope leads to a vantage point surveying the lowlands to the absolute limits of possibility. The traffic rushes north and south on the motorway below. There are houses, farms, factories and stables studding the level plain. Aloft, among the rocks and heather, it is not hard to feel that *Dubhchoire* is a fold in time, so imperceptible that it has survived. Not without threat. It appears to have been ploughed in the not-too-distant past and to have been harrowed recently by motor bikes. According to local legend, the cultivation-ridges or 'lazy-beds' in this shallow valley are remnants of the potato-famine.

The enclosure itself is surrounded by a thick earthen rampart faced with stone. Traces of at least a dozen small huts were found within, during an excavation in the 1930s, and there is evidence of an associated field-system.

Ringforts – there are thousands all over Ireland – were not generally intended to be defensive. They were the enclosures in which farm-families built huts and kept their livestock at night. Although some date from the Iron Age, they belong mainly to the early Christian period, (AD 400–1200). *Lios an tSeagail* might have been used until comparatively recently for 'booleying', the summer grazing of cattle in highland pastures.

 # TRUMPET HILL

The brown bull was captured, of course. He escaped, was recaptured and dispatched towards Connacht. Time was running out; the Ulstermen were about to arise from their labour pains.

Medb's army moved south from the Cooley Mountains, and the journey home began. Cuchulainn, still alone, took a stand on top of *Ochaine*, known today as Trumpet Hill, a rocky eminence clad in beech trees, overlooking Dundalk Bay. He hurled stones at the retreating army from the hilltop, killing so many men at night that the terrified soldiers were afraid to go about alone and went to the toilet in great bunches, presenting an even easier target. Medb herself was forced to take shelter under a barrel-shaped swathe of shields held aloft by half the army.

Cuchulainn maintained his onslaught after they had put Dundalk behind them. 'Not one man in three escaped without his thighbone or his head or his eye being smashed, or without some blemish for the rest of his life.'

The Connacht army limped across the River Fane at *Ath dá Ferta*, Ford of the Two Graves, near Knockbridge on the

R171 today. This is about five miles inland from the mouth of the river where Cuchulainn had killed Medb's two pets on the journey north. The battered army camped at last in *Crích Rois*, which is the broad plain between the River Fane and the River Dee.

DUEL AT ARDEE

It was from this campsite just north of Ardee that Ferdia was sent forth to fight Cuchulainn in single combat. The two heroes were foster brothers, one of the closest of all relationships in Gaelic culture. Medb had bribed and tricked Ferdia into the fight, offering her daughter as a reward. To break his continuing resistance, she plied Ferdia with drink, reverting to her role as the 'goddess who intoxicates'. He did not yield until she claimed in public that Cuchulainn had insulted his prowess. With that twist of Medb's tongue, single combat at the ford of Ardee was launched between the champion of Ulster and the Connacht hero.[5]

The dramatic power of the episode comes from the emotional bond created between the two heroes. After a bad start when they goad each other with disappointed insults, the brutality of the struggle is underscored by the kind of mutual love that Yukio Mishima, the twentieth-century novelist, celebrated among Japanese warriors. It is a physical and a mystical bond that comes from living on the edge of the sword, in the light of glory and the shadow of death. To kill one another is their professional duty and the ultimate challenge to their skill, but the more their bodies merge in blood and gore in the ford at Ardee, the more they love the traditional oneness that they are. Aristotle, in the fourth century

BC, reported that the culture of Celtic warriorhood was openly tolerant of homosexuality. Relations between warriors and women in the Táin have no trace of the tenderness with which Ferdia and Cuchulainn minister to each other's wounds at night. Their love for each other is the heart of the brutal saga; their duel is the most famous episode of the Táin – and yet it is known to be a recent addition, dating from the ninth or tenth century, and not part of the original at all.

On the fourth day of combat, Cuchulainn found the viciousness to perform a foul stroke and to overcome their unity. He hooked the barbed *ga bolga*, a unique weapon, out of the water with his foot and kicked it up into Ferdia's crotch so that the spear entered between his buttocks and drove straight up into his bowels where it opened out into thirty points.[6] Ferdia's dead body had to be butchered in order to extract the weapon. Cuchulainn's act amounted to a savage, symbolic rape. As a betrayal, it is perhaps surpassed only by his slaughter – in another story – of his own son. He used the *ga bolga* on that occasion too, bringing the boy's entrails down around his ankles. Those who portray Cuchulainn as a shining hero might bear in mind that his most extreme acts of savagery were intended to impress the king of Ulster with his absolute loyalty.

Pursuit through Co. Westmeath

The Ulstermen were on their feet. A horde of heroes led by Conchobar, their king, poured from the northern province in pursuit of Medb's army. Their coming shook the forests and drove the wild animals out onto the plains. The breath of the warriors filled the valleys with a fog so dense that the hills looked like islands in a lake. The uproar of their travel thundered through the land. Delays for single combat had ensured that the retreating army would be caught. An advance foray came upon Medb's rearguard at a ford on the River Brosna, just to the east of Mullingar, relieving them of their heads and of the women they had kidnapped in the Cooleys.

Medb sent back an observer who saw men and horses instead of hills and slopes all the way from Ardee to Mullingar, a distance of more than forty miles. The vengeful Ulstermen skidded to a halt at *Slemain Midi*, a smooth plateau a couple of miles northwest of Mullingar. The ancient name is preserved in the modern Slanemore (big, slick place). There the Ulstermen set up their war camp overlooking Lough Owel. The quality of the landscape and its pleasant elevation is emphasised by a variety of burial mounds, staking a claim to the airy plateau from the earliest times.

In the morning, the soldiers rushed naked into battle. Those whose camps faced the other direction burst out through the backs of their tents in their rage to fight. They had a few miles to travel because the battle erupted further south in a place known to the Táin as *Gáireach*, and as Garhy today. Close to Lough Ennell, it lies along the R390 from Mullingar to Moate. Well beyond the suburbs of Mullingar, the rumpled landscape is attractively undeveloped. It is studded with ringforts in various stages of extinction.

Fergus mac Róich of Ulster, fighting for Queen Medb, came up against a former friend on the battlefield. 'You rage very hard at your kith and kin,' the warrior sneered. 'For the sake of a whore's backside.'

Cuchulainn, his body riddled with wounds, joined in the slaughter, and massacred all before him. After an attempt on the life of his former king was deflected, mac Róich and his Ulster exiles left the battlefield rather than dishonour themselves any further. The Gaileoin of Leinster and the men of Munster also withdrew. The battle lay between Ulster and Connacht alone. Medb's army suffered a savage and a well-deserved defeat. They fled to the Shannon, crossing this time at Athlone. Medb bewailed the shambles of the retreat to her former lover. Fergus made his bitter response: 'We followed the rump of a misguiding woman. It is the usual thing for a herd led by a mare to be strayed and destroyed.'

 # BATTLE OF THE BULLS

The journey moved into metaphor as *Donn Cuailnge*, the brown bull, met *Finnbennach*, the white-horned, and the battle of the bulls broke out. *Donn*, in myth, was the force of darkness, and *Finn* the power of light. The battle raged the length and breadth of Ireland under cover of night, until the white bull was slaughtered and his mangled remains were hoisted on the victor's horns. The dark bull staggered northwards, strewing the landscape with portions of his foe. As each body-part hit the ground, the landscape received a matching name. The liver, *ae*, fell at Cruachain Ae. *Luan*, the loins, landed at Athlone. *Láirig*, the thigh, gave its name to Port Láirge, Waterford today. And Dublin, or Áth Cliath, was named for *cliatha*, the ribs. This conclusion is not one of the finer moments of the Táin. It is *Dinnseanchas* (place-lore) out of control. The brown bull, a carcase impaled on his horns, suggests nothing so much as a berserk forklift careering countrywide, a pallet of beef aloft on the prongs.

The Cattle-raid of Cooley is a rear-view mirror on a violent past. The Pagan Iron Age of the Táin – a few centuries spanning the birth of Christ – is a shadowy period, fraught with hardship. As a race, we do not remember coming through there. (Many of us joined the bloodstream and the memory bank a long while after.) Maybe we disowned those origins in the light of the Christianity that followed. The ingrown darkness will have gone on taking toll, exacting blood money for the past, no matter how far we move away. Time, for us, has been a rising series of coils, repeating circles, playing out conflicts. We have not lifted far above the early spirals, and the past is still the future if we slip back down a notch.

We live at the scene of the crime, and the flashbacks have not ended yet.

Brian Boru

(1006)

No other Irish ruler, before or since, travelled as vigorously as Brian Boru. Kingship was to wind down wearily soon after his reign, as if he had worn out the mechanism. Upstart king of a minor Irish tribe, he grew in power a thousand years ago to dominate the entire island. A master of military and political strategy, he challenged the ruling dynasty for the high kingship. Reigning at the end of the Viking period, he was killed in old age at the Battle of Clontarf.

Brian Boru was so mobile throughout his life that travel became a major theme in the folklore celebrating him. A young woman was said to have walked the length of Ireland on her own, from Tory in the northwest to Glandore in the

IRELAND

Tory Island
Fair Head
Aranmore Island
Coleraine Dál Riada
Cenél Conaill
Strabane
Foyle
Cenél nEoghain
Ulaid
Barnesmore Gap
Uí Néill (Northern)
Lower Bann
Dál nAraidbe
Ballyshannon (Assaroe)
Lough Neagh
Drumcliff
Benbulben
Armagh
Dál Fiatach
Sligo
Erne
Newry
Lagan
Achill Island
Gap of the North
Clew Bay
Magh nAí
Uí Néill (Southern)
Slyne Head
Boyne
Dublin
Dublin Bay
Galway Bay
Athlone
Shannon
Dál Cais (Tuamumu)
Aghaboe
Laigin
Loop Head
Magh Adhair
Kincora
START
Limerick
Osraige
Nore
Barrow
Slaney
Eoghanacht (Desmumu)
Cashel
Dingle Bay
Blackwater
Carnsore Point
Lee
Suir
Hook Head
Bandon
Kenmare Bay
Bantry Bay
Mizen Head

BRIAN BORU
Tour of the North 1006

Route of Brian Boru | Viking Town | Church | River Crossing

far south, during his reign. She flaunted a rod in front of her, with a gold ring mounted on it. The story symbolised the peace and prosperity of the great king's reign, and was meant to reflect well on his descendants. The annals give a more accurate image, though, of a period clotted with medieval violence. The young woman with the ring is more appealing to folk memory than the prisoners who made harrowing journeys in and out of the country at the time, as part of a booming slave trade.

 MARCHING KING

Self-imposed king of an ungovernable Ireland, in his sixties, Brian Boru ranged powerfully around the country from Kincora, his base at Killaloe in Co. Clare. He patrolled Ulster in particular, clockwise and anticlockwise, as if he intended to tread the province into submission. The tour of the north in 1006, made at the age of sixty-five, was a show of strength, a triumphant procession from Kincora, taking hostages from all the unruly tribes of Ulster to consolidate his power.

At the age of seventy, he launched a two-pronged approach on the Donegal area, his ships sailing up the Atlantic coast while his army went north by land. He captured the King of Cenél Conaill and brought him back to Co. Clare as a hostage. Brian's eldest son, Murchadha, his right-hand man, also raided Donegal that year and took, according to the annals, 'three hundred captives and many cows'.

Some of Brian's journeys might be seen as ritual flourishes, the excursions of a man who could not sit still, even in old age. But the intention, in his later years, was to dominate the tribes of the northern Uí Néill, who had traditionally provided every second king of Ireland, alternating with the Uí Néill of Meath. Brian, an outsider, had smashed that chain and was intent on forging a new one. Murchadha, his son, was to be the second link.

At the age of seventy-two, Brian marched into Osraighe, (roughly Co. Kilkenny today) and spent three summer months punishing it for defiance. He pushed on to Dublin in September, and besieged the city for a further three months, without gaining entry.

He travelled the long road from Clare to Dublin again the following year, 1014 – one way only this time. Given the average life expectancy at the time, he was more than halfway through a second life by then. Seventy-three-year-olds did not go raiding around the medieval countryside as a rule. The stones and mud of the roads would lock a man's joints at an early age, whether on horseback or on foot, while the scars of battle would strangle flexibility. Perhaps Brian was spared the normal penalties of age. A diet of fish from the Shannon estuary would have helped in that respect. There were other exceptions; Máel Sechnaill, the Uí Néill King of Ireland who was Brian's rival and sometimes ally, was his match in ways.

Máel Sechnaill, later known as Malachy, used the military march as a jab into the midriff of an enemy. He was defensive too, building a barrier of stone across the River Shannon at Lanesborough to block the body punches launched upstream by Brian Boru.

 # PROPAGANDA

Brian died at the Battle of Clontarf, on Good Friday, 1014, hacked to death in his tent by a Viking called Brodir, from the Isle of Man. Many of the popular tales of Brian's kingship come from *Cogadh Gaedhel re Gallaibh*, an account of the Viking wars in Ireland, written over a century later. Composed as propaganda, 'The Battle of the Irish against the Foreigners' is responsible for Brian Boru's reputation as the greatest king of Ireland before or since. It was not the only account. The *Brjanssaga* from the Norse Chronicles also gave Brian Boru a heroic dimension while relating the events at Clontarf from the other side. The Saga reported that Brian's severed head knitted itself back to his body after the attack. Strong on anatomical detail, it described the fate of Brodir, the king-slayer, when Brian's people captured him. 'They cut open his belly and led him round and round the trunk of a tree and so wound all his entrails out of him, and he did not die before they were all drawn out of him.'

It contained flashes of humour too, along with the surgery. Thorstein, one of the Norsemen fleeing towards the longships moored off the shore, stopped to tie his shoe-strings. About to behead him, Brian's grandson wondered why he was not in a hurry. 'I won't get home tonight,' Thorstein said. 'I live in Iceland.'

 # ORIGINS

Brian Boru was born at the tail end of a sprawling family. His father was petty king of a medieval group, based to the north of Limerick, on the Shannon. Of obscure origins, they had recently adopted the name Dál Cais (Dalcassians), echoing an ancient king. In a fiercely elitist culture, they had no future without a royal past. A suitable lineage was forged.

The family occupied a couple of forts in the area of

modern Killaloe. Kincora, the fort fondly associated with Brian himself, has disappeared. One theory is that it stood on the hill overlooking the Shannon, where the Catholic church of Killaloe stands today. Béal Boru still exists outside the town. It was a ringfort of the kind traditionally known as a *ráith* (or *rath*): a circular embankment with a cluster of thatched dwellings within. The wooden houses were fiercely combustible. Fortified with a palisade of bristling stakes, Béal Boru overlooked the Shannon. It is thought that there was a ford on the river at that point. Dál Cais were in a position to control travel and trade at strategic points, such as the Falls of Doonass at Castleconnell, where boats were portaged along the banks. Boru, *Boroimhe*, was not a surname. It was a cattle tax, paid to the occupants of the fort. (A couple of centuries after the death of Brian Boru, the Normans developed the site into a defensive mound.)

The wider region of Brian's birth was Tuamumu, Thomond or North Munster. His people were traditionally a minor force in the overall province, controlling Clare, parts of North Tipperary and East Limerick. There are hints that Brian's grandfather, Lorcan, may have considered himself King of Munster during a hiccup in the reign of the Eoghanacht, the ruling dynasty. Brian's father, Cennétigh, certainly did not reach the throne, but he did the best he could and married into another one. The daughter of the King of Connacht gave a transfusion of royalty to his sons.

Orlaith, one of Brian's older sisters, was well placed in the court of Donncha, the elderly King of Ireland. His fourth wife, she was effectively a concubine. She may have missed her step in the dark, because she was found in her stepson's bed, and was executed. That was AD 940, a year before Brian was born.

By the time Brian had reached early manhood, an older brother, Mathgamhain (Mahon), was King of Thomond. Like a Clare hurling team, Mathgamhain and Dál Cais were not rated for the Munster title, and that made them doubly dangerous. The Eoghanacht had kept the title to themselves for centuries and assumed they owned it. But Dál Cais, the minor power, were primed and going places. Their rivals in Munster were in disarray. On the broader stage, the Uí Néill had been over-kings of Ireland for centuries, with the southern and northern factions taking it in turns to provide the King of Ireland: *rí Éireann*.

The Viking invasions and wars of the previous hundred and fifty years were largely over by then. The Northmen had settled in towns, which they developed around the Irish coast, including Dublin, Waterford and Cork. Close to Dál Cais territory, Limerick was a major Viking outpost, a port on the Shannon estuary, a trading centre. Like Dublin, it was surrounded by new agricultural development.

The population of Ireland in the tenth century was about half a million, although some estimates are a fraction of that. Many areas that are populated now were undrained bog or heavy woodland then. Apart from the nobles and the landless poor, the inhabitants were mainly cattle-breeders and mixed farmers. The equivalent of today's 'strong' farmer was the *bó-aire* who lived in his own ringfort and was a snug man.

 # GUERRILLA WARFARE

Cogadh Gaedhel, an account written over a century later, insists that Brian Boru spent some of his early manhood in the wilderness, on the Clare side of the Shannon. Estranged from his brother Mathgamhain, the tribal king, he waged guerrilla warfare on the Vikings of Limerick. The theory is that he learned to fight like the Danes, learned the use of their weapons and developed a sense of military strategy. Usually dismissed as folklore and propaganda, the story at least has the merit of making him learn the hard way.

> Great ... were the hardship and the ruin, the bad food and bad bedding *(droch chuid ocus do drochlebaid)* inflicted on him in the wild huts of the wilderness, on the hard knotty wet roots of his own native country.

Brian is said to have adopted the battleaxe of the Vikings over a clumsier Irish model. He may also have favoured the longer and heavier sword they used. Any such change would not be an individual choice, however. It had more to do with an improvement in the techniques of Irish blacksmiths who imitated the sophisticated Viking weapons. The Irish sword was a short stabbing-tool, for intimate use. It could be wielded in either fist; a busy warrior could handle two. But the longer Viking weapon could have kept an Irish swordsman at bay. The Irish were also partial to a light spear or javelin with a line attached. There are differences of opinion as to whether the line was for retrieval, or was wrapped around the shaft to give a spinning action. It may have served both purposes, although the latter seems a bit esoteric for close combat.

In terms of strategy, Brian Boru's main innovation was the use of a fleet to intimidate the provincial Irish kings, by delivering troops to the back door. This was nothing new. For a century and more, the Vikings had taken large fleets, heavily manned, up the major rivers, including the Shannon, the Liffey, the Boyne and the Erne, plundering the inland monasteries with devastating ease. Brian constructed a fleet of longships based on the Viking model. The boats, built of overlapping timbers, had a shallow draft for river use, and were unstable, but they were capable of sailing easily inland. The fleet was augmented by traditional hide-covered boats and the all-purpose dugout canoe. In one raid, Brian is reported to have mustered three hundred boats on Lough Ree, a lake on the River Shannon.

Attempts to block his passage with barriers of stone across the river were futile. Máel Sechnaill and the King of Connacht built barricades at Athlone and Lanesborough, each working out from his own bank.

As his brother grew in strength to become a challenger for the Munster title, Brian became his lieutenant and put his military skill to good use. This is clear from the defeat of the Limerick Vikings, a victory the brothers pulled off between them. Brian's capacity to remain on the move was clearly demonstrated.

 SHOWDOWN

The rout took place in 968, at Solohead, a little north of the present Tipperary town and a long day's march from Limerick. Not only were the Vikings thrashed in a battle that lasted from sunrise till noon, but Brian and his men continued the slaughter on the run, and then pulled off an all-night march to take Limerick by surprise at dawn. Every male of military potential in the city, including boys, was put to death on Singland Hill.

❧ *Slave Trade*

After the Singland massacre, said to have been orchestrated by the twenty-seven-year-old Brian, a chilling event is described in *Cogadh Gaedhel*:

> … a great line of the women of the foreigners was placed on the hill of Singland in a circle, and they were stooped with their hands on the ground, and marshalled by the horseboys of the army behind them, for the good of the souls of the foreigners who were killed in the battle.

The author is anxious to emphasise Brian's Christian credentials after the savage slaughter. But horseboys were not church stewards. They were famously an uncouth rabble. While the image seems to represent an organised scene of mourning, it carries stronger echoes or intimations of rape, always a weapon of war.

Certainly these women, many of them slaves already, would be taken and traded as forced labour by the army of Mathgamhain and Brian Boru. The use of prisoners of war as slaves was a normal feature of medieval Ireland, with a major trade at home and abroad. The female *cumhal*, so familiar in the ancient texts and translated by nineteenth-century academics as a 'bondmaid' instead of a slave, represented a measure of currency, the equivalent of cattle or ounces of silver. Female slaves did heavy domestic work, especially milling duties with grinding stones.

It was to be a proud boast of Brian's reign that:

> … no son of a soldier, or of an officer of the Gaedhel stooped to put his hand to a flail, or any other labour on earth; nor did a woman deign to put her hand to the grinding of corn, or to knead a cake, or to wash her clothes, but had a foreign man or a foreign woman to work for them.

HEAD TO HEAD

Due to the paralysis of his rivals and the strength of Dál Cais, Mathgamhain became King of Munster in 970. Violent death was inevitable. He survived a surprising six years, before he was fatally stabbed. Brian, at the age of thirty-five, unchallenged, took the hurdles in his stride. In 976, as King of Thomond, he smashed the Eoghanacht. A couple of years later, he took the crown of Munster.

Now he was an upstart threat to the kingdoms further east – to Leinster, to Meath, and to the Uí Néill over-kings of Ireland. Waterford shook its fist. Brian lashed out. A long, forced march, and all of a sudden he had hammered the Waterford Irish and the local Danes, and he had their ally, the King of Leinster, by the throat. He imposed a savagely contemptuous tax on the province. Three years after becoming the backwoods king of minor Thomond, he was nominal ruler of the southern half of Ireland.

At that same moment, as if fate conspired towards a great all-Ireland final, Máel Sechnaill, ruler of Meath, became the Uí Néill King of Ireland. He controlled, in effect, the northern half.

It was dog-eat-dog for awhile. Máel Sechnaill marched all the way cross-country from Meath to Thomond and urinated on Brian's royal mound at Magh Adhair. In fact, he uprooted the ceremonial tree, but it was the same gesture. Then Máel Sechnaill attempted to take control both of Leinster and of Viking Dublin. In a move owing something to chess, he married the exotic Gormfhlaith, mother of Sitric, King of Dublin. To add to her charms, her brother was soon to be King of Leinster. As a strategy, it was a tempting alternative to Brian's forced marches and punitive taxes, and Brian was to learn from it. He too would marry Gormfhlaith and gain control of Dublin.

In the meantime, Brian showed a trick he had learned from the Vikings. He put a fleet of ships on the Shannon and sailed upriver, taking the surrounding country under his control. In passing, he ravaged the kingdom of Meath, effectively pissing on Máel Sechnaill's tree.

Various options were open to this pair of well-matched kings. They could leap into immediate conflict, annihilating one and leaving the other fatally weakened. That was standard Irish practice. Alternatively, they could hold off and build up strength – before resorting to the first option. Brian sailed up the Shannon again, put three hundred boats on Lough Ree and defeated Connacht. Máel Sechnaill took Dublin under his control. They had stopped urinating on each other's trees, and now they were massing pieces at opposite ends of the board. Meanwhile, Leinster and Dublin, hostile to them both, were gagging for a chance to revolt.

QUEEN OF INTRIGUE

There was a third option open to the kings. They could form an alliance against common enemies and achieve a balance of power. In the year 997, in good time for the millennium, they did precisely that; Máel Sechnaill in good faith, Brian with a stone up his sleeve. Together they smashed the eastern alliance of Dublin and Leinster. Had the two kings been even more imaginative, they might have left their armies aside and marched against Gormfhlaith, the queen of intrigue. Sensing that Brian was the coming man, she had turned her son and her brother against Máel Sechnaill. He repudiated her and Brian moved up in the queue.

The harmony of the kings was short-lived. Brian seized the upper hand when the spoils of Dublin were divided out. Then he married Gormfhlaith – not because he needed a wife, but to tighten his grip on Dublin and Leinster. It is unlikely that Máel Sechnaill attended the wedding. Or that a Connacht lady called Dubhchobhlaigh was among the guests. Brian was still married to her, his third wife, and she would remain his queen until her death in 1008.

Gormfhlaith was fifteen years Brian's junior. There is a tendency to think that she was beautiful, but she didn't have to be. It was all about connections. Even if she had once been attractive, she was in her mid-forties then, not a medieval lady's finest decade. These marital alliances were as much part and parcel of medieval kingship as celebrity weddings are part of show business today. They were a strategic alternative to giving battle. War in medieval Ireland was expensive, destructive, seasonal and undermanned. It was seldom the sports tournament of popular imagination.

Having married Gormfhlaith (he was her third husband), Brian made it a belt-and-braces job by marrying his daughter to her son, Sitric, King of Dublin. He had a reserve of daughters for such functions. With Leinster and Dublin defeated, Brian and Máel Sechnaill could have settled into ruling the country in two halves. Ireland was divided conveniently by a ridge of gravel running straight through the midlands from Dublin to Galway. This feature, the *Eiscir Riada*, had been deposited with political accuracy by the last receding glaciers. Tides of bog washed up against it on both sides. It had always provided a high and dry route across the country, fording the Shannon south of Clonmacnoise.

However, Brian was not satisfied with half of Ireland. The stage was set for the battle of the big kings.

Shortly after taking control of Dublin with Máel Sechnaill's assistance, Brian turned on his royal ally and led an army into Meath, his provincial kingdom. In this attack on the established King of Ireland, Brian Boru was assisted by a troop of Viking cavalry. Folk history has conveniently forgotten this. It must have given great satisfaction to Máel Sechnaill to cut the legs from under this impertinent attack and to watch Brian Boru retreat.

However, it was no more than a setback, and Máel Sechnaill was being undercut in every direction. Typical, though, of Brian that when he was defeated, it was a troop of expendable Vikings he sacrificed.

 # POWER SHIFT

In 1001, Brian made a military move into the northern half of the country, marching to Dundalk where an extraordinary standoff with the armies of the northern Uí Néill occurred. He did not attempt to break their blockade. Neither did they attack. It was as if Brian's campaign carried the force of change, and the Uí Néill were blunted by centuries of presumption. Riddled with internal feuds, they underestimated the threat to their entire dynasty. A year later, when Brian demanded the abdication of the King of Ireland, Máel Sechnaill's kinsmen did not back their man. Unbalanced from within, the Uí Néill had begun to topple.

Máel Sechnaill was left with nothing but a kind of piercing dignity which exposed all the more clearly the baseness of his kin. He stepped aside, and it is as if a gap was suddenly created that allows us to look back at the squabbles of the Uí Néill at the very moment when they sank from supremacy after centuries of power.

A body of myth has grown up around Brian's response,

arising mainly out of *Cogadh Gaedhel*. The two kings face each other on the plains of Meath, the proud Máel Sechnaill pared back to a petty king through no fault of his own. Noble in his loss, he hands over the crown of Ireland. To the amazement of the multitude, Brian Boru hands it back and offers him another year to recover his support and to defend his throne. It is no more than propagandist fiction from the twelfth century, designed to reflect well on Brian Boru and to clear him of the charge of usurpation.

Brian Boru did not hesitate to become King of Ireland in Máel Sechnaill's place – *almost* King of Ireland. No one would ever dominate the entire island. Or, to put it another way, the entire island would never unite under a single authority. Squabbling kings and lords would remain the norm.

 # BRAWLING KINGS

Ruling from Cashel in Munster, Brian was limited in what he could do with the north; he launched a series of journeys so frequent as to create an illusion of constant presence. He would never fully subdue the brawling kings and, in reality, he was a long way from being the sovereign ruler of an island united in peace and Christianity, as hagiography would have it.

Brian involved himself throughout Ireland in Church affairs, funding construction and resolving disputes. Frequent tours called on the hospitality of monasteries, and a visit must have been money in the bank. An older brother, Marcán, had accelerated through the clerical ranks with Brian's support to become a high-ranking abbot. He was a useful filter when it came to moral judgements on his brother's actions.

❧ Road-building

Leaving aside the claims for Brian as a builder of monasteries and churches, he has a serious reputation for road construction. So too has Cormac Mac Airt, a mythical king of early Ireland, reputed to have been responsible, in the second century AD for the Five Great Roads. Legend has a simple filing system, and the virtues of one great king were automatically ascribed to another. Great kings built roads. Or kings who built roads were great.

Brian's road-building was not philanthropic; it was a function of his military journeys. He had an efficient engineering corps, an advance troop skilled in clearing obstacles on the rough tracks that formed a network throughout Ireland. The old law tracts make great work of the Irish roads, defining them in detail according to status, function, and width. The reality is likely to have been a miserable mess. There was the *slighe* or main road, of which five radiated out from Tara. However, as with Tara itself, this was a notional rather than a national institution, referring to general routes heading in the main directions. It does not mean a star-shaped set of paved roads slicing into the provinces.

There were varying degrees of lesser road, with the *bóthar* or cow track being of the lowest order. It was meant to be wide enough by law to allow for the passing of cows without injuring each others' calves. This was defined as the width of two cows – one lengthways, the other at a right angle. It was further ordained by Brehon Law that those dwelling alongside them should keep roads in good order. It is hard to imagine that such notions could have been enforced. Roads in medieval Ireland were glorified tracks. While hospitality was a legal obligation, it was not in anyone's interest to make it easy for an enemy to arrive on the doorstep. At the same time, kings and overlords made annual rounds of their subjects and were accommodated and entertained. This process would be known as 'coshering' by the time it reached the sixteenth century as a lavish vice and a crushing burden. It is safe to guess that tenants of all kinds scrambled to clear the tracks when such visits were due.

Brian knew that the Church, unlike a kingship, could not be taken by force. Whether or not it could be bought was a very different question. He concentrated on the princes of the Church, particularly in the north where they were under the patronage of the Uí Néill. He confirmed the primacy of Armagh, a major monastic force in Ulster, rather than switching that power to the south. The weight of his influence might be measured against the twenty ounces of gold Brian left on the main altar at Armagh during one of his journeys through the north. Such skilful devotion did not impede his cause. Good relations with the clergy eased his dealings with regional warlords, who were often their kin. He would shortly see himself inscribed in the Book of Armagh as *Imperator Scottorum*, 'Emperor of the Irish', a breathtaking pretension. On his death, his body would be conveyed in solemn pomp to Armagh and buried there.

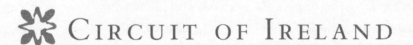 CIRCUIT OF IRELAND

Brian tramped north in 1005, 1006, 1007 and 1010, to secure his hold on a defiant Ulster. The removal of the Donegal king to Kincora in 1011 might be interpreted as a kind of rescue mission, a strategic kidnap. Not only would it give Brian control of that territory, but it might also be in the king's own interest, safeguarding him from internecine strife. Challengers to his throne would hear the echoes of Brian's recent presence and sense the threat of his return. It would be difficult for any faction in Donegal to seize power, as Brian's own people, Dál Cais, had done in Munster. It was not difficult for Brian Boru to anticipate his enemies – he himself had been that enemy.

Brian Boru's Tour of the North in 1006, or his Circuit of Ireland, as it came to be called, was his most elaborate journey. His army gathered at Athlone, and he travelled up the Shannon from Kincora to meet them there. The hosting (an assembly for a military campaign) was composed of detachments of soldiers called in from allies throughout the southern half of Ireland. The numbers were swollen by levies of part-time soldiers available between the spring sowing and the harvest. They marched north through the Roscommon plain, *Magh nAí. Aí* refers to sheep, and so the common epithet, 'Roscommon sheep-stealers' probably goes back a long way.

Brian Boru whipped on northwards, crossing into Sligo, the lands of Connacht tribes Uí Ailella and Cairbre. The ancient pass of the Curlew Mountains, between Connacht and Ulster, makes no impression in the modern landscape, traversed as it is by an EU-funded strip of tarmac. Only a rusting horse and a Gaelic Apache mounted above the roadway mark an important junction with the past.

 # Bed and Breakfast

It is not hard to visualise the army of Brian Boru as being on a kind of holiday as it approached the mountains and the beaches of the Sligo coast, taking in the sights, collecting guests along the way. That these were hostages does not mean that they were all ripped from their homes and dragged along in chains. It is more apt to think of them (young princes perhaps of the petty kingdoms) as pledges of loyalty whose experience of Brian's court and hospitality would reinforce the alliances of their fathers.

There were no brawls along the way to disrupt the holiday atmosphere. Although Brian could be chillingly lethal, he was also a man of discipline and order. The army passed Drumcliff where there was a church of Colmcille. Brian would, of course, make donations along the route, taking monasteries and churches under his protection. By that simple and perhaps sincere device, he could establish a circuit of moral approval to match the political network he was extending. Monasteries were required by law to offer Bed & Breakfast. This is often seen as a quality of Gaelic character – our traditional generosity – but it was a practical means of ensuring accommodation for travellers, usually the *aes dána*, the intelligentsia and the craftsmen who moved freely around the country. Brian Boru, though, would have camped with his army wherever possible. It is a common trait of warrior-kings and successful generals that they are most comfortable with their troops and that this closeness breeds a loyalty, which is fundamental to their success.

Travelling with him, Brian had his own personal poet, Mac Liag, the man thought by many to have written *Cogadh Gaedhel*, although it was actually composed long after his death. As they rode along the Sligo coast, the Atlantic surf broke against the beach at Streedagh and the headland at Mullaghmore, while the great cliffs of Slieve League would have been visible across the bay to the north. Some of the Clare men might have made anxious comparisons with the Cliffs of Moher. A thousand years before Yeats made Benbulben famous, Brian Boru and his poet – horsemen – passed by. The English language was still to come. The lyrical language of Ireland was passing one of its high points and turning purple on the lips of sycophantic bards. The language of *Cogadh*

Gaedhel is clogged with grease, but an epitaph for Brian rings with the resonance of the earlier tongue.

> *… nir ba cloch ininad ugi fein, ocus nir ba sop ininad largi, acht ba tren ininad trein, ocus ba tend iar tend.*

> He was not a stone in the place of an egg, and he was not a wisp in the place of a club, but he was a champion in a champion's place, and he was valour after valour.

SLIGO-LEITRIM

The route north followed the coast. It struck west of King's Mountain, passed under the prow of Benbulben, and soon left the sharp ridge of Benwiskin behind, propping the limestone plateau against the sky. That was the recognised way, the alternative being the bogs and lakes of Leitrim. Brian was following a corridor of fords and passes that led from one territory to the next. At one stage of the itinerary outlined in the annals, he seems almost to take flight like a boy careering along, arms outstretched:

> … into the country of Cairpre, and beyond Sligech, and keeping his left hand to the sea and his right hand to the land and to Beinn Gulban over Dubh and over Drobhaois and into Magh-n-Eine, and over Ath Seanaigh at Easruaidh; and into Tír Aedha and over Bearnas Mór, and over Fearsad and into Tír Eoghain ….

The rivers Duff and Drowes (*Dubh agus Drobhaois*) were crossed, the first flowing out of the steep-sided cleft of Glenade, the second draining from Lough Melvin. Neither would have presented any problem to the engineers if the bridges were down or the fords up. They are not big rivers. The Four Masters, annalists of Brian Boru, would themselves be closely associated with the Drowes, six hundred years later. They compiled their major work, at a secret location on its banks. Today the two rivers mark the limits of the Co. Leitrim coastline – all three miles of it.

Further inland, towards the foot of the limestone rampart, a straggle of Early Medieval homesteads stretches all the way from Sligo along this section of Brian Boru's journey. These ringfort dwellings, widespread throughout Ireland, were in general use between the fifth and twelfth centuries. They were not fortifications, as we tend to assume. Neither were they fairy-forts, a belief that helped preserve thousands of them in later years. They were farmsteads – the standard homes of the better off. A raised circular bank contained the house and outhouses. The embankment offered rudimentary protection for the cattle-farmers who occupied them. Stone walls and thorn fences kept the animals secure. The dairy business seems to have been thriving during this period, though perhaps not as gloriously as legend proclaims.

Sadly, that decade was little different from any other, to judge by the annals. Death and destruction flourished. Cenél Conaill, Cenél Eoghain, and the Ulaid, all the major powers of the north, were at each others' throats – or rather Cenél Eoghain was at the throats of the other two, ranged on both sides of it. The Annals of Ulster, 1004, record wholesale slaughter. Kings to the left and right – Ailech and Dál nAraidhe – were killed by Cenél Eoghain, whose own king had hoped to succeed Máel Sechnaill as *rí Érenn*. In the same year, Máel Sechnaill 'fell from his horse, so that he lay mortally ill'. Few men were of sufficient note to merit a provisional obituary in the Annals. In the light of such turmoil, it is not difficult to understand why Brian felt the need to impose his presence repeatedly on the province.

DONEGAL

Crossing the River Erne at the ford of Ballyshanny (*Béal Átha Seanaidh*) on his major circuit, Brian rode on to previously forbidden ground. He'd been blocked there two years before by the northern tribes, temporarily united by his visit. However, in 1006, the way was clear, a tacit submission in itself. Had it been blocked a second time, Brian would have cleared it, at great cost to the northern groups. There was no need to chase Cenél Conaill, the clans of Donegal, into their own highlands; they handed over their hostages and Brian veered northeastwards to face down the other faction, Cenél Eoghain.

The Barnesmore Gap is a gigantic vee, slashed deep and direct through the flanks of the Blue Stack Mountains. It cleaves into otherwise inaccessible terrain. Boulders and bog along the bottom would have forced the old route higher than the bed of the pass. The original line must have traversed the slope, though not necessarily as high as the line of the abandoned railway today. The river below, beside the modern road, traces so many oxbow bends that the eye is tempted to read it as a watery script.

At first sight, the long funnel of the gap looks ideal for an ambush from the granite outcrops overhead. But the slopes are too steep, too long, too rough underfoot. Soldiers would not so much hurtle from above as tumble head over heels, looking foolish on arrival. Ferns and heather on the damp hillside make it an ideal breeding ground for midges. There is no way of knowing whether our ancestors suffered from midges as badly as we do today. Perhaps modern hygiene leaves us more exposed, without a protective layer on the skin. But washing is not an entirely recent habit; hot water on arrival was a condition of Early Medieval hospitality. Maybe there was a midge repellent based on some herb or ingredient we no longer eat. Today, there is only one effective cure for the Donegal midge: a mixture of cow dung and paraffin smeared on the skin – and set on fire.

In any event, there was no ambush. Cenél Eoghain was not fighting back. Obviously the weight of power was on Brian's side, the northern tribes riven and fractured. Taking pledges from them, he marched on to cross the River Foyle at the ford of Strabane. How did a royal hostage from Donegal get on with one from Tyrone (Cenél Eoghain) in the cavalcade of the Munster king? There is no record, but the same match would occur almost six hundred years later when Red Hugh O'Donnell from Donegal and Art O'Neill of Tyrone were locked up in Dublin Castle as hostages of the Crown. Despite the enmity of their factions, they escaped to embark on a journey together that has linked their names in brotherhood forever.

❋ ULSTER

Marching close to modern Coleraine, Brian crossed the River Bann in the vicinity of Camus where a monastery marked the ford. Far from being hidden and remote, most monasteries occupied important crossing points in the landscape. They were focal points and often trading posts. Brian swung into North Antrim, and then veered sharply south towards Belfast Lough. This corner of Ireland was the territory of the Ulaid, once enormously powerful (in the era of the Táin), but now pushed aside by the expansionist Uí Néill. The Ulaid gave their name to Ulster. Their most northerly faction, Dál Riada, had previously colonised western Scotland in the early centuries of the first millennium, seeding the Gaelic language there.

Brian took in Dál nAraidhe too, the Ulaid kingdom centred on Belfast Lough. There was no hint of the city of Belfast then, not even a monastery around which a town might cluster. (Belfast began, from scratch, in 1603.) Passing Co. Down and the Mourne Mountains, he took pledges of good faith from Dál Fiatach, the grouping which tended to monopolise the over-kingship of the Ulaid. It was very much to his advantage that all these factions were at war with the Uí Néill, particularly with Cenél Eoghain. In a recent battle between them, when the Ulaid were badly defeated, there had been '… a slaughter of the army, both noble and base … as well as the elite of Ulster', according to the local annals In fact, it could be said that Brian picked the ideal time to lord it over the north – a period of years when there was hardly a warrior left standing on his feet.

At the end of the summer, Brian and his army emerged from the northern kingdoms through the 'Gap of the North'. This pass, midway between Newry and Dundalk, was the eastern portal of the province. Today it marks the border between the Republic and Northern Ireland. When Queen Medb of Connacht attacked Ulster in the Iron Age saga, Táin Bó Cuailnge, she marched all the way across the midlands in order to approach via the Gap of the North. All the heroes of Ulster were flat on their backs suffering under a mysterious curse. Ironically, the same might be said of them in 1006, except that there was no mystery; the curse was division. But Ulster was usually defended by the complexity of its landscape. Its natural boundaries – hills, bogs and lakes –

set it apart from the rest of Ireland, so that the alienation we struggle with today is in many ways as old as the hills.

Brian Boru's Tour of the North, 1006, was not unlike an invasion of another country. As if in acknowledgement, *Cogadh Gaedhel* rushes on to attack Scotland and England immediately, stampeding Brian into an action he did not actually take. Many thought he might. His determination to be King of Ireland and the attribution in the Book of Armagh to Brian, Emperor of the Irish have combined to form a strong belief that his ambitions extended beyond the island of Ireland to some kind of western empire. It is inevitable that such a concept would have been imagined, based on the pattern of Charlemagne in Europe, but Brian Boru was still a long way from achieving the stability in Ireland required to support a wider vision.

The successful campaign of 1006 was traditionally presented as a Circuit of Ireland, although it included neither Munster nor Leinster, and largely skirted Connacht. But Brian's army included troops from all those parts and provinces. In marching first to Athlone, and then homewards from the Gap of the North, some of the army at least could be said to have completed a plausible Circuit.

 # CLONTARF

Over the next few years, Leinster and Dublin would continue to wrangle and conspire, eventually forcing the Battle of Clontarf in 1014. Brian himself, at the age of seventy-three, would be killed on the fringe of the battle, after the moment of victory. So too would Murchadha, his son and likely successor. Murchadha's son, Brian's grandson, would also die. While many still see the Battle of Clontarf as the final defeat of the Vikings in Ireland, the fact is that they had long been absorbed into the country and were not at all the threat they had been up to a century before. But the Battle of Clontarf would put an end to any illusions of an Irish empire ruled by a royal dynasty descended from Brian Boru.

Máel Sechnaill, who had fallen from his horse with such a thump that the shock was felt in the annals, had recovered. A long-suffering ally, he withdrew his support on the eve of the Battle of Clontarf, leaving Brian's largely Munster army severely tested. Máel Sechnaill became *rí Érenn* again on Brian's death and ruled until 1022.

From then on, for a century and a half, the descendants of Brian and those of the Uí Néill would struggle for supremacy. While the Uí Briain, as they came to be known, were usually in the dominant position, they would never again reach the eminence achieved by Brian Boru. A century and a half after his death, the arrival of the Normans would begin to alter forever the kingships and the balance of power in Ireland.

IV

THE HALO &
THE SWORD

6 Warrior and Saint
Caoilte and St Patrick
(5TH CENTURY AD)

*callamh na Seanórach,* Discourse of the Elders, is the story of a journey around Ireland made by St Patrick and a pagan warrior of the Fianna, Caoilte mac Rónáin. Set in the fifth century AD, the account was written in the twelfth century. *Acallamh,* a compilation of Fenian lore, is the overarching narrative of medieval Irish literature. Episodes from the journey have become the staples of Irish folklore; its characters and their adventures have gone on to influence world literature.

The old pagans and the new Christians had not merged easily in the fifth century. Although Ireland as a whole converted to Christianity, war bands had continued to exist, and

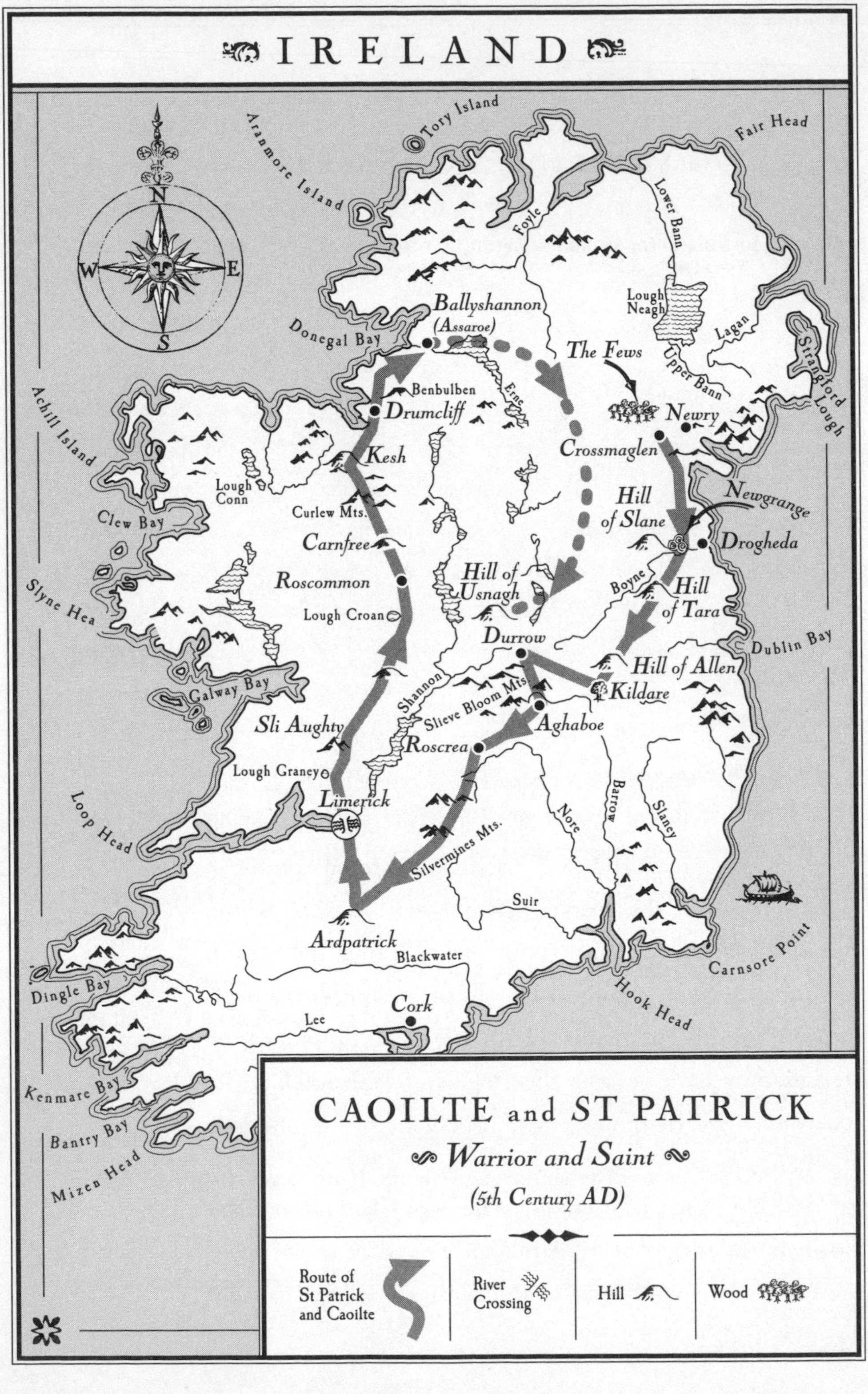
IRELAND
N
S
E
W
Tory Island
Aranmore Island
Fair Head
Foyle
Lower Bann
Lough Neagh
Lagan
Upper Bann
Strangford Lough
Ballyshannon
(Assaroe)
Donegal Bay
The Fews
Benbulben
Drumcliff
Erne
Newry
Achill Island
Kesh
Crossmaglen
Lough Conn
Hill of Slane
Newgrange
Curlew Mts.
Clew Bay
Carnfree
Drogheda
Roscommon
Hill of Usnagh
Boyne
Hill of Tara
Slyne Hea
Lough Croan
Durrow
Dublin Bay
Hill of Allen
Kildare
Galway Bay
Shannon
Slieve Bloom Mts
Aghaboe
Sli Aughty
Roscrea
Lough Graney
Limerick
Nore
Barrow
Slaney
Loop Head
Silvermines Mts.
Suir
Ardpatrick
Carnsore Point
Blackwater
Hook Head
Dingle Bay
Cork
Lee
Kenmare Bay
Bantry Bay
Mizen Head
CAOILTE and ST PATRICK
Warrior and Saint
(5th Century AD)
Route of St Patrick and Caoilte
River Crossing
Hill
Wood

❧ St Patrick and the Fianna

St Patrick is a verifiable, historical figure, born in Roman Britain, a missionary to Ireland in the fifth century AD. Son of Calpurnius, a deacon, and grandson of a priest, Patrick was captured as a youth near the west coast of Britain and was enslaved in Ireland for six years. Later, he returned as a missionary to the land of his captivity and spent the remainder of his life in Ireland. He is believed to have worked mainly in the east midlands, but tradition has attributed to him virtually all the efforts and achievements of the early missionaries.

Fionn mac Cumhail, Oisín, Caoilte and the rest of the Fianna are not fantasy figures either. They are the heroes of a real warrior culture from the final chapter of pagan Ireland, when the aggressive kingships employed roving bands of mercenaries for military purposes. Such units were known as *fiana*. They contained men of noble birth, still to come into their inheritance; younger sons squeezed out of power; and other elite victims of dispossession. Some were outlaws, swords for hire; others were adventurers; some were loyal to a master – on call to their king. The subversive force of their warrior culture was such that the *fiana* were later romanticised to become, in the popular imagination, the legendary Fianna, or Fenians, led by Fionn mac Cumhail.

Fleet-footed, broad-chested and deep of lung, they travelled on foot, free of chariots and the elite trappings that characterised Celtic culture in the European style. It was nothing to the Fianna to run down stags and boars in the forest, to stride into battle or step it out to a feast a hundred miles away.

They lived in the wilderness and revelled in it. Their dress was a linen tunic, the *léine*, and a woollen cloak, the *brat*. A sense of simple freedom ensured their popularity forever. Any barefoot boy running in a field at any time in Ireland could imagine himself a Fenian warrior.

Just as various war bands and their local movements were fused by folklore into one continuous surge of Fenian travel, so the ripples of many evangelists became the singular marathon of St Patrick.

their adherents were branded 'sons of death' by the early Church. Both bodies – the war bands of the Fianna and the missionaries who succeeded them – had a tradition of hard travelling, on foot, through the same terrain. St Patrick, as he appears in this medieval itinerary, composed long after he lived, is not the politically correct figure we know today. This is not the patron saint of the plaster statue – mitred and croziered, grave and measured, dressed up in a green gown, throttling a snake. The Patrick of *Acallamh* is at once a clever magician and a cunning diplomat, practised in local politics, founding a Church on the joint platform of principle and wealth.

In the modern idiom, *Acallamh na Seanórach* would be a road movie, with Patrick whipping the journey along on the righteous energy of his mission. In the long-established literary tradition of the road genre, the saint's sidekick is his tragicomic opposite – a pagan, a broken-down warrior, whose loyalty humanises the saint's mission. Caoilte has the shambling presence and the clear wit of the Wise Fool.

Their journey and its landscape are vividly detailed, at once fantastical and recognisable. There are time-shifts and diversions, up mountains and down into the Otherworld. Covering the entire country in a set of dashing forays, *Acallamh* is the first great travel guide to Ireland.

The landscape releases a flood of stories. Every landmark, every place name on the journey sparks questions and the travellers light up with tales – of battles, love affairs, hunts, feasts, treachery, loyalty and humour.

ROADS AND FORDS

The elaborate circuit of Ireland walked by Caoilte and St Patrick is ornamented with provincial loops and cross-country stitching. At times, the travellers follow the Five Great Roads of ancient Ireland, which were simply the main directions to and from the provinces, with a notional focus on Tara.

Routes throughout early Christian Ireland were not mysterious, as they have often been portrayed. They were networks of tracks such as might be found in any remote landscape today, worn into existence for pastoral and sometimes for military reasons. As might be expected in a cattle culture, many of them were herding trails. They connected major fords and causeways, sometimes following the crest of an esker (a ridge of moraine), a route hewn through woodland, or a wooden gangway (*tóchar*) over a bog.

SOUTH ARMAGH

The journey began in south Armagh when two ancient warriors, Caoilte and Oisín, stumbled from the forest of the Fews. There was a small problem at the outset. Caoilte and Oisín had been wiped out with Fionn and the rest of the Fianna long before St Patrick arrived in Ireland in the fifth century. The story took that disjunction in its stride without the convenience of a bridge. They were dug up and pitched forward in time to fit the plot. Loose teeth and old bones rattling, sinews snapping, the characters simply heaved into view one Christian morning in the Fews Mountains. Accompanied by a few retainers, they appeared, not as heroes locked in their monotonous prime, but as vulnerable ancients deserving respect and pity. Charged with grief for a lost culture, they embodied the heroic life of the pagan senses, and its cruel decline.

The Fews (*fíodh*: a wood), from which they emerged rheumy-eyed into a new order, was one of the great 'black holes' of the Irish landscape. West of Slieve Gullion and stretching from today's Crossmaglen to Newry, it was a ruggedly wooded area in south Armagh where time (and law) barely prevailed. Today the name itself has almost disappeared with the forest, but a little of the character remains. Full of hidden places until the helicopter came, the Fews was famously resistant to hostile outsiders. It was an ideal lair for a remnant of the Fianna, just as it would be a bolthole for outlaws through every century that followed, down to the present day.

Plodding from Armagh into Co. Louth at the start of a journey into another culture, the old diehards were soon on the major route south that links Newry, Dundalk and Drogheda today. The landmarks were painfully familiar – mounds and ridges everywhere, strewn with abandoned stories. The stripped silence made memory all the more intense. Woods were felled where they had hunted; the forts and dwellings of their kind were swept away. They did not understand this new country where they had their bearings and yet were completely lost. Here and there were wooden structures with strange emblems; men with shaven heads hurled incantations at them.

Slieve Gullion, the Cooleys, the Mournes – haunts of the old hunters – diminished behind them in the distance. They felt huge, clumsy and very old in a world of smaller men. Before their journey's end, all but two of their retainers

⁊ The Myth of Fionn mac Cumhail

From modern analysis of tradition and the development of myth, it appears that the warrior Fionn mac Cumhail acquired the visionary qualities of *Find*, a much earlier figure, to become in the process an enduring hero of enormous power. *Find* embodied the wisdom of a Celtic deity of the Boyne Valley, preceding the cult of the *fiana*. Fionn mac Cumhail, absorbing him, was to become the hero of a later culture.

In early Christian Ireland, Fionn became the avatar (god as man) of a Leinster tribe, Uí Fáilghe, whose boundaries had been compressed by the Uí Néill in their expansion out of the Boyne Valley. Fionn mac Cumhail, originally borrowed from the Boyne, became a symbol of their struggle.[1]

would 'put their mouths to the ground' and perish from loneliness and old age.

They were the last of their kind. The great men they served, their leader Fionn mac Cumhail, their friends and fellow warriors, sons and grandsons were all dead. They plodded down the flat coastal plain towards the River Boyne. Where the Christian tradition would later distinguish itself with Monasterboice and Mellifont, both in ruins today, the geriatric warriors swung right along the river, heading west.

RIVER BOYNE, CO. MEATH

This was *Slí Mhidluachra*, the ancient route from Tara to Ulster. Tara, *Temhair* in Co. Meath, was the political centre of early Ireland – insofar as there was one – where the concept of overkingship was focused. The warriors were travelling the route in reverse, going south towards the Boyne and west towards the Hill of Slane.

Oisín disappeared on Otherworld business, leaving the sorrowing Caoilte to continue the journey. Their parting was as of the soul from the body. The heroic emotion was rather exaggerated, since Caoilte was still accompanied by nine retainers, and anyway Oisín was to reappear for a later episode of *Acallamh*.

Bereft, Caoilte visited first the Pool of Fiacc at Rosnaree on the Bend of the Boyne (close to the megalithic tomb at Newgrange and a traditional fording point on the river.) This was the place where Fionn, his beloved leader, had burned his finger as a boy and – sucking it – had tasted the Salmon of Knowledge, which gave him the power of second sight.

HILL OF ALLEN, CO. KILDARE

Moving upriver, Caoilte stopped neither at the Hill of Slane nor the Hill of Tara. Those great sites were steeped in traditions of their own and would distract his journey. He was heading for the Hill of Allen, near Newbridge in Co. Kildare today, where it stands between the River Liffey and the Royal Canal. Originally a sacred site, it was known as *Almhu*, centre of the powerful Leinster cult of Fionn mac Cumhail. The Hill of Allen was both his home and his burial mound.

Today this great landmark has been hollowed out by quarrying, and a large part of the hill has been removed, although the noisy summit can be reached from a point close to the little village of Allen. On the level of respect alone, it

❧ The Fenian Lays

Oisín was the son of Fionn mac Cumhail, and tradition accords him a radical response to Christianity. His reaction is found in the subversive medium of the Fenian Lays, *Laoithe na Féinne*. These verse tales were carried in the oral tradition right through to the twentieth century, smuggled like contraband under the tongue. 'I don't like your Mass,' Oisín warns Patrick. 'I want nothing to do with you.'

The notion of Oisín telling Patrick where to get off has appealed to an anti-clerical streak hoarded in the popular imagination for centuries. Many verses, rarely printed or translated, exist.

Cuirim druim leatsa, a Phádraig
I turn my back on you, Patrick,
Is go lá an bhráth leis an gcléir,
And reject forever your priests,
Agus fós le Neamh na n-órd
Likewise your ordered Heaven
Is le slóighte uile naomh.
And all its ranks of saints.

When Fionn and the Fianna lived
They loved the hills, not
monkish cells.
Blackbird song is what they loved;
Not the harsh sound of your bells.

If my son Oscar and your God,
Were in combat on Cnoc na bhFiann,
If I saw my son knocked down,
I'd admit God is a strong man.

It would be an almighty shame if God
Would not release Fionn from flame,
For if God himself were in Hell,
Fionn would fight in His name.

is perhaps little wonder that motorways and roads built from the rubble of an ancient landmark should be so destructive of human life.

Caoilte, once Fionn's loyal lieutenant, was on a

pilgrimage to the past. He tramped up to *Almhu*, and stumbled into a brand new future. No quarrying then, as far as we know, but Patricius, son of Calpurn, had arrived; he was scattering demons in every direction, blessing the mound, claiming it for a new god. Pledged to defend his culture to the death, Caoilte might have sprung into action and routed this new druid, but instead he was strangely passive. Humbly he accepted the baptism rained upon him. He was in the hands of a Christian author, of course.

Caoilte avoided confrontation. To pay for his baptism, he reached into the rim of his shield and handed over a bar of gold. Religion would be an expensive business – he could see that. However, the Christian saint was not enforcing prayer or reviling feasts. The Adze-head, *Tálcheann*, as Patrick came to be known, was a lively character with whom it might be a challenge to travel.

Camped companionably on the Hill of Allen, the missionaries fed their pagan guests; they elicited heroic tales, admired the finer points of Fenian life, and condemned nothing. For the moment. The old man came out of himself in Patrick's skilful hands. Having cleared the problem of profanity with his attendant angels, the saint ordered that Caoilte's words be written down as treasures for posterity. What old warrior could resist that compliment? The questions too were designed to swell his heart with honest pride.

'What has kept you warriors alive for all these years?'

'The truth of our hearts, the strength of our arms, and the constancy of our tongues.'

'Was your leader a good man?'

Caoilte left Patrick in no doubt on that score:

'Were the dark leaves gold that the trees let fall,

With the silver wave, he would give it all.'

His blood quickened, nerves thrilled; he was himself again. 'Sixty were the queens following in my wake; in truth I was a rogue, and yet I pleased them all.'

A nervous moment for the Christians. Monogamy was their platform. 'Is our dinner ready yet?' Patrick harrumphed.

 # COOKING

Food for the missionaries was provided by their wealthy converts – kings and cattlemen in the surrounding landscape. Patrick extended the hospitality to Caoilte and his men, and they chipped in the fruit of their own labours. For nomadic hunters, the most effective means of cooking raw meat in a hurry, even today, is to cut it in strips and roast it over a bed of hardwood embers in a shallow pit.

The modern landscape and its maps are dotted with *fulachta fiadh*, timber-lined pits designed for boiling water with hot stones. These are traditionally associated with the feasting of the Fianna, but there is now considerable doubt that they were ever used for cooking; they belong to much earlier Bronze Age settlements.

 # STORYTELLER

Caoilte's first tale boasted of the bravery of the Fianna. Nine of the leading warriors, including Oisín and himself, had raided Britain once to recover some stolen hounds. With a white shield on each man's shoulder, two stabbing spears in each right hand, and a helmet on every head, these nine were the equal of any four hundred warriors in the world. They brought home their hounds and a herd of the finest horses as well.[2]

The raid on Britain brings Niall of the Nine Hostages to mind, a semi-historic Irish warrior said to have captured the young St Patrick while on a slaving raid. He is reputed to have ravaged as far afield as the European Alps in the fifth century. He may well have been the leader of an actual *fian* in his time.

While Caoilte's tales proved over and over the courage of the Fianna, they reflected at a deeper level an obsession with personal honour and renown, to be maintained by violence. They pointed also to the brutal insecurity of a society in crisis, as pre-Christian Ireland appears to have been, leaving it open to convulsive change. And it is obvious too from the constant celebration of drunkenness and all its fetishes – particularly the ritual drinking-vessels of the Fianna – that a sacramental drink culture is lodged right at the earliest roots of Irish identity.

In between Caoilte's stories, Patrick made some crucial conversions.

'You shall have the kingship tomorrow at the middle of the day,' he promised a dispossessed prince. 'And your race after you.'

But Patrick had second thoughts: 'Unless you turn against the Church.'

The religious future of the east midlands thus secured, it was time to move on and tackle Munster. Patrick and his new bodyguard headed southwest.

KILDARE AND OFFALY

Just as Caoilte's approach had followed the logic of an ancient route, *Slí Mhidluachra* to Tara, the next leg is loosely associated with *Slí Dhála*, the route from Tara to North Munster. Stepping off the Hill of Allen, they made their first stop in Kildare. *Cill Dara* (church of the oak) suggests the pagan cult of Brigit, goddess of animals and fertility, which would have been familiar to the Fianna and was widely known throughout Celtic Europe. The oak in the place name may be an echo of a sacred tree or grove on the old site. Within a century of Patrick's presence, the goddess Brigit would be transformed into the Christian saint, Brighid or *Bríd*. She was given a back-story in later Christian lore, making her a member of the Uí Fotharta, a group coming to power just then among the Leinstermen. Ownership of the goddess-saint must have given them a fine head start.

Afterwards, Patrick and Caoilte continued, in the words of *Acallamh*: 'by the Wood of a River-Branch and the Ridge of Clay, now called the Church of the Oak, across the river-pool at Durrow, across the ever-green River Barrow, and over the Causeway of Líag, daughter of Cúarnatán ....'

In other words, the route from Kildare took them south over the River Barrow, past the Slieve Bloom Mountains, through the plains of Laois and over the headwaters of the River Nore. This was wet and rugged country, not easy ground to travel in the early Christian era when it was the tribal territory of Uí Fáilghe. The rivers were forded, some-times waded, and narrow necks of bog were crossed by wooden causeways (*tóchair*), some of which are still pre-served in the peat of Offaly today. The tribes and their lands tended to be separated from each other by natural features of the landscape – forests, bogs, rivers, uplands. This added to their sense of independence.

Travel in the low-lying midland bogs had not become much easier by the time *Acallamh* was compiled in the late twelfth century. Ó Conchobhair Fáilghe held the area at that period as an island in a sea of Anglo-Norman expansion, indi-cating that access was still difficult.

Between Aghaboe (site of a later monastery) and Roscrea, the warrior and the priests were briefly on *Slí Dhála* and the main road to Cashel. Hard travellers, they did not stay on it long, veering west from Tipperary into Limerick instead. The popular story of the visit to Cashel when St Patrick nailed the king's foot to the floor with his crozier, did not arise on this journey.

❧ The Politics of Legend

When *Acallamh* was being compiled from the oral tradition in the twelfth century, there was intense competition for the Munster kingship between the O'Brien descendants of Brian Boru and a rival dynasty. The author had to strike a careful balance as to which dynasty he placed in power seven hundred years earlier. The king who visited Ardpatrick was not an O'Brien. As far as it went, this was historically correct, since the royal pedigree of Brian Boru was a very stunted tail indeed.

The Rock of Cashel, a great Munster landmark, may have been excluded from the journey because it might have identified *Acallamh* too closely with one faction of the later struggle for power.

❋ ARDPATRICK, CO. LIMERICK

The travellers took their next break at the foot of a hill – not just any old lump in the landscape, but the one still reputed to be the highest green hill in Ireland. *Tulach na Féinne*, as it was called, or the Hill of the Fianna, (185 metres), is a green jewel clasped in the dark bezel of the Ballyhoura Mountains. Neatly conical, grassed to the summit, it seems to control by natural right the tracts of grazing that stretch north towards Limerick, the finest dairy land in Ireland. Patrick is said to have founded a church on top, and the hill is now called Ardpatrick. Like many a prelate, he had an eye for a prime site. That church was followed by later churches, all in ruins now, and by a round tower of which only the butt remains. One of Ireland's airiest graveyards sits on the summit, still in use though slightly neglected, as if the height of the hill puts it just above regular attention. A walk on Ardpatrick gives a pleasant uphill stroll into the past, with views over the present, and the future almost in sight.

Caoilte recalled how the Fianna, on that very hill, had feasted on berries and hazelnuts, bramble-shoots, sprigs of gentian, roasted birds, salmon and eel. O'Sullivan Beare and his followers tramping north from west Cork in the winter of 1603 were to slide deep into starvation as they camped at the foot of Ardpatrick, finding only a little watercress in the surrounding countryside. Throughout history, travellers and storytellers are drawn to the same significant landmarks which feature repeatedly in the accounts.

The saint and the warrior did not go hungry. They were met there by the King of Munster and his nobles, who laid their heads in Patrick's lap – a gesture of submission – and rewarded him. 'Patrick stayed there for a week, raising the dead, and curing sickness and disease of every kind.' More Messiah than missionary, he certainly out-miracled the pagan druids who could not quite raise the dead. Witch-doctors and shamans often roused people from induced trances, but not from the grave.

As soon as Patrick had converted the nobles and nailed down the little mountain for the future Church, Caoilte secured it for the pagan past. A poor bargain, but the odds were against him. He told a lame story of the naming of the hill by the Fianna as they left it on their way to the Battle of Ventry. 'This is a lovely hill,' remarked Fionn. 'What better name so,' said his men, 'than the Fair Hill!' Caoilte recovered from that low-point to relate the great tale of the battle itself, one of the most poignant episodes in the Fenian tradition.

The early Christians were deeply touched by the tragedy of Caol and Crédhe. 'May you have victory and blessing,' said

❧ *The Battle of Ventry*

An invasion force had arrived at Ventry Strand on the Dingle Peninsula in west Kerry, even as the Fianna were feasting on their hilltop in Limerick. It was led by Dáire Donn, King of the World. Setting off from Fair Hill to repel the invaders, the Fianna diverted in order to help a young comrade to win the woman he loved. He was Caol and she was Crédhe, a lady of high standards from the Paps of Anu, twin hills in Co. Kerry dedicated to a goddess of the land and renowned for their suggestive symmetry.

The entire cohort of the Fianna struck south from Ardpatrick towards Killarney to support Caol, instead of racing west to Dingle to confront the invasion. Caol had to present his case in a poem composed for Crédhe. Countless suitors had fallen at this hurdle, and the Fianna were doubtful of his chances. But his foster mother was an insider; she had composed his poem for him.

The wedding lasted a week, the couple in a well-appointed bed and the Fianna roistering. The full poem is in *Acallamh*.

Crédhe came to the battle with the Fianna to support her new husband. She brought her herds to sustain the warriors, the small black Kerry cows that still survive today. Cattle would be kept at a discreet distance from the fighting. Capturing the enemy's herd was one way of ensuring victory.

The Battle of Ventry, famous in Fenian lore, was a savage affair lasting seventeen days. Crédhe supplied the Fianna with milk throughout and tended to the wounded. Her husband, on his honeymoon, fought more fiercely than any of his comrades. On the last day of the battle, chasing an opponent into the sea, he was drowned and his body came ashore with the tide. Heartbroken, Crédhe lay down beside him and uttered a piercing lament in verse. When it was complete, she died of sorrow. The lovers were buried in a single grave at Ventry, and it was Caoilte himself who raised a monument in stone above their heads.

This story belongs to the later lore of the Fianna and it was composed well into the Christian period. Ventry was chosen for the battle, not for any historical reason, but because some storyteller felt the White Strand of the name would set off a blood-red battle rather well.

Patrick. 'The story you have told is a good one. Where is Broccán, our scribe?'

'Here,' said Broccán.

'Then write down everything that Caoilte recited.'

And he did.

The mood on Ardpatrick changed as a party of local men approached, spears upright like a grove of trees on the move. Although they put their heads in Patrick's lap, it was a passing courtesy, and it was Caoilte they wanted to meet. Could he teach them how the Fianna of old had hunted so that they might smarten their technique? When Caoilte heard how poor their efforts were, he wept for them until both his shirt and his chest were wet. He took them up to a lake in the Ballyhoura Mountains, overlooking Ardpatrick from behind. With his assistance, they caught eight hundred animals. They would not find it as easy now, because the Ballyhouras have been tangled with Sitka spruce for years.

One of Patrick's priests demanded ten per cent of the hunt as the Church's share. The locals were not used to Christian charity and their leader refused. Struck to the ground with vicious stomach cramps, he begged Patrick for relief: 'Put your hand on the pain!' But it was Caoilte, not Patrick, who rounded on him.

'Not till you pay the fee!'

The old warrior turned bully-boy on his own people now that he was Patrick's right-hand man. He even set the fee: the belly of every cow and every pig and every sheep to the Church henceforth, in exchange for the stomach cramps. The victim had no choice but to agree, committing his descendants also to the deal. Only then did Patrick put his hand on the pain.

From that point on, Caoilte's role could easily be read as that of a fundraiser for the Church. He is inclined to be constable and tax-collector too. While there are always locals willing to be jailers and executioners of their own people, it should be remembered whose story *Acallamh* is. It was designed to portray the Fianna as willing collaborators with Christianity. As his journey unfolds, Caoilte opens the graves of his beloved comrades and hands out the contents, the choice share going to the Church. Traditionally seen as generosity to a deserving cause, this reads today as heritage-stripping and grave-robbery. But for all his propensity to act the bully-boy, Caoilte is intrinsically innocent. While loneliness and loss make him devious, a *slíbhín* on occasion, he remains a warrior-poet of the wilderness and a great storyteller.

FERMOY, CO. CORK

Caoilte took a detour by himself from Ardpatrick to Fermoy, a short distance away in east Cork.

Even in these casual asides, the journey tallies with the actual landscape. The author of the compilation must have had personal knowledge of the whole country; perhaps from a tour of Church properties in the twelfth century. The *aes dána*, poets and craftsmen in early Ireland, had travelled the country freely on cultural errands; Christian churchmen continued the practice.

In the stronghold of the *Fir Maige* (the Plainsmen, who gave their name to Fermoy), Caoilte met two grieving sisters married to a pair of brothers who had gone off to get themselves new wives. He took a practical approach, giving them herbs which the women of the Fianna had traditionally used as an aphrodisiac. The problem of the roaming husbands of Fermoy was solved. Those herbs might have been nothing more erotic than bathing scents. A clean fragrance would be an aphrosidiac in a boudoir normally smelling of smoke, half-cured furs and animal fats. Caoilte rewarded himself for his marriage counselling by uprooting an enormous stone that concealed the treasure of a fellow warrior.

Monogamy is one of the fundamental themes of *Acallamh*. A royal wedding is postponed for thirty pages at Patrick's insistence, until the first queen dies. In case the aspirant might hurry things along, Patrick threatens to disfigure her so badly that her own mother wouldn't want to see her.

✍ *Language*

Even in fifth-century Ireland, there must have been traces of the older pre-Gaelic languages still echoing somewhere. We have no knowledge of them. The Gaelic that derived from the European Celts and began to suffuse the country in the Iron Age a few centuries BC could hardly have smothered every word and idiom so soon. The originals of the Fianna, in the third century AD, although mimicking the warriors of Celtic Europe, must have retained something of the unknown cultures that existed before the Indo-European tide washed slowly into Ireland. Today it is accepted that there was no actual Celtic invasion; change was brought about by a process of absorption. Accents, idioms, styles, maybe an older mindset and its pre-Celtic customs, must have lingered in pockets here and there. West of the Shannon maybe, or in upland areas? Would such people, conscious of some earlier loss, have been conservative, more resistant to Christianity? On the other hand, might they not have been more vulnerable to the cultural viruses that new systems carry?

OVER THE RIVER SHANNON

Caoilte hurried back to Ardpatrick and the missionaries headed north, warriors in train, to spread the seed of the Church in Connacht. There was still a strong belief, even in the twentieth century, that St Patrick travelled extensively in Co. Limerick, including an ascent of a hill near Foynes, now known as Knockpatrick, from which he blessed the wide mouth of the Shannon estuary.

The party crossed the Shannon at Limerick itself, which would not really exist until the Viking settlement hundreds of years later. The final fording point on the Shannon was not far away, although it must have been seasonal and extremely limited, given the proximity of the estuary. Ferries (dugout canoes and skin-covered coracles) brought travellers over the river as long as relations between the north and south banks were amiable.

The party moved rapidly northwards through east Clare to *Loch na Bó Girre*, the Lake of the Short Cow, an old name for Lough Graney in the Aughty Mountains. From there they plunged into east Galway through the territory of Uí Maine (to become O'Kelly country in time) and through the wetlands of the River Suck straight to the banks of Lough Croan, between Ballinasloe and Roscommon town. The landscape of the River Suck in the western midlands has a haunting charm quite different from anything else in Ireland. It can be walked by a way-marked route that might call for rubber boots at times but still retains the lonesome character of bog and riverbank and the essence of traditional community.

LOUGH CROAN, CO. ROSCOMMON

Camped at Lough Croan, Patrick and Caoilte sat on a mound overlooking the lake. Caoilte was like a trader in tapestries, spreading out exotic tales for Patrick's benign inspection. Every now and then, a story took the saint's fancy, and he had it written down. They focused on the mound itself, and Caoilte described the burials it housed. At one end was a warrior who had died of shame because he could not instantly reward a poet for a tribute in verse. Refusing to wait, the poet had threatened satire. The warrior put his mouth to the ground and rose no more. Patrick granted Heaven to him for his sense of honour. It was no idle offer; the pagan's soul rose from Hell and hovered as a white dove over Patrick's head. In the other end of the mound lay a famous warrior interred with fifty silver chains ...

Fifty what!? Heads snapped to attention as Caoilte droned on. 'We would be most happy,' purred a cleric, 'to get his treasure.'

Caoilte opened the grave, and raked out the silver armrings with the shaft of his spear.

'You gave Heaven to a man for his honour,' the priest petitioned Patrick; 'Give this man Heaven for his treasure.'

Idly dispensing wisdom and redemption, they passed the day. Meanwhile, the King of Connacht's son dropped dead after scoring six goals in a hurling match. Womenfolk dying of grief prepared to put their mouths to the ground unless Patrick intervened. He used a golden basin and a silver cup to miraculous effect, and soon the whole of Connacht was in his hands. Recovering from the trance of death, the young man sat up 'as if waking after being with a woman or after heavy drinking ....' Some translations leave such details out, as being, perhaps, unsuited to Christian ears. The story continues:

'Laying their heads in Patrick's lap, the Connacht nobles gave their treasures and their goods, their riches and their plunder, their cattle-herds, horses and their horse-teams, their arm-rings and their other wealth into the power of Patrick.'

Those of us who grew up around Lough Croan will agree that riches and plunder were scarce indeed as a result. Arm-rings were certainly in short supply.

The company moved on next morning, passing possibly the little two-roomed school in Scardaun where we sat at our desks. Such was the immediate sense of history and folklore in the 1950s that the Fianna, Brian Boru, Red Hugh O'Donnell, the Black and Tans, were capable of riding by at any time, day or night, hot on each others' heels, followed by headless horsemen and thirteen hearses in a row. Long before television, local landscape was a traffic jam of drama.

Heading due north, the party passed a site known to them as *Ros na Fingaile*, or the wood of the Kin-Slaying, where nine sons of one family had slaughtered each other. Things had quietened down by the time we arrived, and the place was known as Roscommon.

❧ *Kings of Connacht*

As recorded in a medieval account, kings of Connacht received the white wand of royal office on the mound at Carnfree, attended by the nobles and the bishops of the region. An inauguration stone with indentations like footprints stood on top until the mid-nineteenth century. Chieftains had prescribed roles in the ritual. Only Ó Maolchonaire was allowed to stand on the mound with the new king. His job was to present the wand. Ó Connachtáin guarded the gate. A bishop was responsible for the king's horse. It was believed that St Patrick had established the ritual when he crowned a king on his visit.

Carnfree was topical when *Acallamh* was compiled in the late twelfth century. The O'Connors had been kings of Connacht for generations. In that same century, they had wrested the overkingship of Ireland from the O'Briens, descendants of Brian Boru. Rory O'Connor, the last king of Ireland was in power when the Norman Invasion occurred in 1169, not long before Patrick and Caoilte were paired up by the author of *Acallamh* and dispatched on their journey. Rory's brother, Cathal Crobhdearg (the red-handed) was king of Connacht until early in the following century.

✳ CARNFREE, CO. ROSCOMMON

Ahead of Patrick and Caoilte, the journey pointed directly towards *Cruachain* (Rathcroghan), the monumental mounds of Connacht, starting point of Táin Bó Cuailnge and legendary site of Queen Medb's palace. *Acallamh* was far too smart to tangle with Rathcroghan and the Táin. Instead, camp was pitched just south of Tulsk at Carnfree, another ritual focus in the Roscommon landscape. Carnfree too is studded with burial mounds, enclosures, earthworks, embankments, double ditches, ring-barrows and cairns. Rippling under the greensward, they are the pressure points of the past. Carnfree is the Cairn of Fraech, a hero associated with the daughter of Queen Medb.

There were good reasons for choosing this stopping point. It was widely believed that St Patrick had actually visited Carnfree and founded a church there when the place was known as *Selc*. This fits rather well with the pattern of early churches established near great pagan sites. The visit is described by Tírechán, who wrote an account of St Patrick's mission around AD 675, a couple of centuries after the events. Patrician propaganda such as his would increasingly attribute churches to the saint himself. The outline of a much later stone building is still visible on the ecclesiastical site at Carnfree.[3]

On the political front, Carnfree was the inauguration site of the kings of Connacht throughout history. The ritual took place on a mound crowning the highest point of the hill of Carns, just south of Tulsk. Although the hill is no more than a raised plateau, it commands a regal view over the watery landscape of east Connacht. The mound, small in itself, still shows traces of stone-facing and is thought to be a Bronze Age burial cairn.

One of the last stories told by Caoilte before taking temporary leave of Patrick was a tale of social order and disorder. *Fidchell* was the board-game attributed to the Fianna, although it actually belonged to a later age. Guaire Goll, a servant, was one of the keepers of Fionn mac Cumhail's chessboard. He thought himself an expert and had notions above his rank. He challenged a player of noble birth, the warrior Finn Bán, to take him on. Finn Bán was one of the three best chess-players in the Fianna. (Fionn and Diarmaid ua Duibhne were the other two; Caoilte did not rank.)

Guaire proposed a bet of three ounces of gold each for three days' play. At the end of the session, he had not won a single game. Losing his temper, he hurled abuse at his opponent, a king's son. Guaire said Finn Bán was an unskilled warrior, clumsy with his weapons. Finn Bán hit him a smack in the mouth, knocking out three upper and three lower teeth. Guaire collapsed across the chessboard.

When Fionn mac Cumhail heard of the assault on his servant, he took it personally. He ordered that Finn Bán and all his followers be killed. This would launch an internecine war, and not a man among the Fianna would be left standing. They already had a savage split with the Mac Morna faction to handle. Oisín pre-empted Fionn's order and called for a judgement by three wise men. One of them was Caoilte. According to their verdict, wherever Fionn met the servant of Finn Bán, he could strike him with his fist. This was backed up by a gift of gold to Fionn from every leader in the Fianna, as an incentive to call off the war. When the heat died down, it emerged that all of Fionn's servants had been getting above themselves and insulting better men. An oath was taken there and then that servants lacking manners would feel their masters' wrath. The conclusion automatically blamed the servant, rather than the master. No doubt the social homily, like any parable, was aimed at some specific target in its time.

In the lofty setting of Carnfree, Patrick asked if the Fianna had ever imagined the existence of God – a smug question somehow. Caoilte described an event that had happened in a hall near Tara. Two hundred sons of kings and two hundred women with them all died during the night, 'after feasting and pleasure'. The Fianna concluded that there must be a god with the power of life and death over everyone. However, Caoilte mentioned a curious detail in passing – their food had not been prepared where they were, but had been brought in from Tara. They should have checked the kitchen.

PARTING OF THE WAYS

Soon Caoilte announced his departure. He was tired, he said, of being in the one place – a lame excuse, since he had just tramped half of Ireland! He took off on a tour of memory in Sligo and south Donegal, with his personal retainers. He went first to the Curlew Mountains, where every journey from Connacht to Ulster passed, and then to Keshcorran, that distinctive little summit with its cave and cairn, standing aloof from the Bricklieve Mountains. From there, Caoilte struck west for the ocean at Ballysadare and on by Rosses Point and Lissadell to Drumcliff at the foot of Benbulben. Most Irish journeys came, sooner or later, to Drumcliff, to the Ridge of Baskets and the monastery there. The round tower, of which a stump survives, must have been quite new when *Acallamh* was compiled.[4]

BENBULBEN, CO. SLIGO

The elegant mountain of Benbulben has many associations with the Fianna, implicit in Caoilte's visit. It was there on the summit plateau that Diarmuid ua Duibhne, Caoilte's foster brother, suffered a fatal wound in a boar hunt. He was gored to death. Fionn mac Cumhail, a jealous old man by then, allowed him to die, in revenge for the loss of Gráinne who had eloped with Diarmuid.

Caoilte spent a day of mourning by the grave of his beloved comrade, on the summit of Benbulben. It does not really matter that all these stories were composed out of sequence and that Diarmuid was stitched into the tapestry hundreds of years after Christianity had been established. He did not exist in the early lore at all. Nor does it matter that Diarmuid had no desire to elope with Gráinne, who blackmailed him into it. What matters is the whole story, zigzagging through the centuries, accumulating character, motivation and plot. Fionn's failure to save Diarmuid on Benbulben brought a tragic reality to the entire tradition, in retrospect. As human imagination gradually extended the myth, Fionn developed from warrior-god to hero to leader and – finally – to a bitter old man.

With that in mind, could there be any greater loneliness than that suffered by Caoilte on the mountaintop? He was exiled in an alien future, old and weary, reliving a past that had funnelled into jealousy, revenge and death. Even as he sat on Benbulben, his dead comrades – the pagan Fianna – had been condemned to Hell by the Christians. He was reduced to grave-robbing in order to bargain for their redemption.

In the evening, he descended from Benbulben and, with his men, he built a hut for the night, thatched with rushes. He found a boar drinking at a nearby well and killed it with a spear-cast. The entire episode shows the story feeding creatively upon itself. Aware of the gory death of Diarmuid in a recently composed tale, *Acallamh* could not pass Benbulben without having Caoilte kill a boar in acknowledgement. It should be noted too that the mountain was originally called Beann *Gulban*, a word that has the sense of a beak or snout, leading some storyteller, driven by the dynamics of place-lore, to the idea of a boar's tusk. It is a major reason for the choice of that location for the finale of *Diarmuid agus Gráinne*.

THE HILL OF USNAGH, CO. WESTMEATH

Before rejoining the Christians, Caoilte went on to have further adventures on his own, including a sojourn in the Otherworld and a chariot ride through certain sites of the Ulster Cycle, echoing briefly the itinerary of Táin Bó Cuailnge, the Cattle-Raid of Cooley, without drawing on its content. It was a flourish added by the author just because he could. Afterwards, Caoilte travelled south to meet Patrick on the Hill of Usnagh, the navel of Ireland, in Co. Westmeath. The ritual hilltop, 181 metres high and just west of Lough Ennell, was said to mark the place where all five provinces came together in a poetic concept that defies geography.

On the summit of Usnagh, Caoilte felt socially exposed.

He was surrounded by great kings and bishops. No one of lesser rank was allowed to enter. 'I am not entitled to sit beside a king,' he said. 'For I am the son of a humble warrior.' A touching democracy broke out for once upon the Hill of Usnagh, and the ancient hero was prevailed upon to take a place of honour beside the King of Ireland.

It was not long before he was telling yarns again. He described how Ireland had once been divided between two kings – the partition agreed on that same Hill of Usnagh. One king, he said, got all the treasure and the wealth, the houses, the cattle and the feasts. The other got nothing but the woods and wilds, the hunting and fishing of hills and rivers. The kings and bishops listening were horrified by this unfair division. Caoilte stood his ground.

'The share that you condemn,' he said, 'is the one that we preferred.'

Perhaps he should have walked away on that exalted note and kept on walking. But he was to travel many roads with Patrick yet. The end of the journey, wherever it was to be, is missing from the manuscripts. Those pages are gone. It may be that Caoilte is still wandering the country, invisible to our domestic eyes, stirring up the wind and the weather, rousing strange waves in his wake, travelling that wild share of the land that no longer exists for those of us who took the houses.

7 TOWARDS THE ANNALS OF THE FOUR MASTERS

The Travels of Michael O'Clery (1626–36)

ntil very recently there were old men in Ireland who went to sleep at night repeating the names of the Four Masters. My own father did. It was a kind of cultural mantra after the normal pieties were done. *Mícheál Ó Cléirigh agus Cúchoigcríche Ó Cléirigh, Fearfeasa Ó Maolchonaire agus Cúchoigcríche Ó Duibhgheanáinn.*

Recollecting them on the verge of oblivion was an

☙ IRELAND ☙

To France

Fair Head

Tory Island

Aranmore Island

Foyle

Lower Bann

Carrickfergus

Lough Neagh

Lagan

Donegal Abbey

Donegal Bay

Bundrowes

Upper Bann

Lough Melvin

Erne

Carlingford Lough

Lough Allen

Achill Island

Clew Bay

Fergal O'Cara
(Patron of the Annals)

CENTRAL PLAIN

Drogheda

Slyne Head

Inny

Multyfarnham

Boyne

Rosserilly
(Bishop of Elphin)

Killinure

Dublin

Galway

Athlone

Brosna

Liffey

Dublin Bay

Galway Bay

Shannon

Ballymacegan
(Home of
Flann MacEgan)

Kildare

Castlekevin

Gort (Cill Chaoide)
(Home of Conor MacBrody)

Barrow

Leighlinn

Ennis

Quin

Nore

Slaney

Loop Head

Limerick

Cashel

Clonmel

Suir

Wexford

Carnsore Point

Blackwater

Hook Head

Dingle Bay

Lee

Cork

Kenmare Bay

Timoleague

Bantry Bay

Mizen Head

ATLANTIC

TOWARDS
❧ THE ANNALS OF ❧
THE FOUR MASTERS
Locations Visited (1626 – 1636)

Town | Castle | Franciscan Friary or Abbey

With acknowledgements to Fr. Brendan Jennings

acknowledgement of what the Four Master themselves had achieved. They were thought to have gathered up Ireland's ancient learning and to have formed it into an ark which they floated on the darkness, just as the seventeenth century eclipsed the country, and memory seemed on the threshold of amnesia. Gaelic culture was not actually on that dark threshold then – it still isn't – but the perception that it was lasted hundreds of years

The Four Masters were the historians who compiled *Annála Ríoghachta na hÉireann*, the Annals of the Kingdom of Ireland. They were two O'Clerys from Donegal, one of the Roscommon Conrys, and a Duignan from Leitrim. The work came to be known as the Annals of the Four Masters. Their names are not commonly known, which added urgency to my father's gesture of remembrance. We don't hear suburban mothers calling Cúchoigcríche (hound of foreign parts) in for his tea and his history homework, and it is unlikely that we will. The name is translated as Peregrine, which adds no glamour although it catches the sense of pilgrimage in the original. And Fearfeasa (man of knowledge) is still a little dodgy for a boy, even in an age when presumption seems a natural right.

 # BROTHER MICHAEL

The Franciscan lay brother, Michael O'Clery, who was to be chief among the Four Masters, travelled exhaustively throughout Ireland in the years leading up to the compilation. He was engaged in continuous research. Travel at the time was difficult and dangerous, although the opening years of the reign of Charles I (1625–41) were not quite as grim in

❧ *Annals of the Four Masters*

The annals (AFM) are a compilation of Irish legend and history from the Year of the Deluge, or Noah's Flood, to AD 1616. The Four Masters were chroniclers rather than historians in the modern sense. Their material consists of dated entries laid out in chronological order, providing a diary of major events from the coming of Ceasair to Ireland forty days before the Flood with fifty girls and three men. Early entries are terse or cryptic:

> Lughaidh Sriabh nDearg, after having been twenty-six years in the sovereignty of Ireland, died of grief.

That was shortly before the birth of Christ. On the other hand, AD 1014 has an eloquent account of the Battle of Clontarf, while the Battle of Kinsale reads like the eyewitness account that it probably was.

The Annals of the Four Masters recorded the major events of an elite culture and its ancient civilisation, its victories and defeats, the comings and goings of its kings, chieftains, abbots and bards. The natural calamities and disasters are there:

> AD 684 – A mortality upon all animals in general throughout the world, for the space of three years, so that there escaped not one out of the thousand of any kind of animals.

And in the same year, not unconnected:

> A great frost this year, so that the lakes and rivers of Ireland were frozen; and the sea between Ireland and Scotland was frozen, so that there was a communication between them on the ice.

Benign windfalls, much rarer than calamities, are recorded too – such as great seasons of milk and crops of beech-mast that fattened all the pigs of Ireland. Much of the early material is legend parading as fact. In more recent times, the work is naturally partisan, recording Viking, Norman and English invasions from a perspective of increasingly battered Gaelic pride. When it came to ordinary people, Irish historians were as elitist as their counterparts elsewhere, and the lower classes were faithfully ignored. The only place they make an impact is on the battlefield, where the casualties are almost always exaggerated. In death, the peasants are much larger than life.

Kept by the hereditary historians of ambitious families, annals were often customised vehicles for propaganda. But it should be remembered that they formed just another strand in the knowledge of the past, augmented by genealogy and *Dinnseanchas*, the lore of place, as well as bardic poetry in which events were ornately recorded.

Compiled during the period 1632–6, manuscript sets of the Annals were circulated for centuries. An edition published 1848–51 in six massive volumes (plus a seventh as an index) runs to well over four thousand pages. This is still the classic version. Edited by the Gaelic scholar John O'Donovan, it contains text and translation on facing pages, and his detailed commentaries as footnotes. These go a long way towards providing the informed background against which the Four Masters worked. O'Donovan has often been referred to as the Fifth Master.

Ireland as often depicted. With the dislocation of the Gaelic system of nobility and patronage since the Nine Years' War and the Flight of the Earls, libraries and manuscripts were increasingly rare.

O'Clery was an hereditary historian, trained in the tradition in Ireland. His family served the O'Donnells, chieftains of Donegal, in that role. He called himself explicitly 'a chronicler by descent and education', *dar duthchas agus darb foghlaim croinic*.

Born in 1590, in Donegal, O'Clery passed his childhood and youth during an intense period of rise and collapse in the fortunes of Gaelic Ireland, including the Nine Years' War, the Battle of Kinsale, and the Flight of the Earls.

Born Tadhg Ó Cléirigh, he was nicknamed 'Tadhg an tSléibhe', Tadhg of the Mountain. He took the religious name, Brother Michael, when he joined the Franciscans. Nothing is known of his early years until he surfaced obscurely in Europe, around 1620, as Don Tadeo Cleri in a note which records a grant of two Spanish crowns monthly on account of 'persecution and loss of estate in Ireland'. There were numerous Irish emigrés and refugees astray at the time in France, Spain, Italy, and the Spanish Lowlands where the Franciscans had established a training-college at Louvain. (This is the present-day Belgium, then under Spanish rule.) The movements of these Irish exiles were observed by English agents on the Continent.

 ## Stolen Saints

A major function of the college was to send help to the 'afflicted Church in Ireland' and to counteract the doctrine of the Protestant Reformation. Members of the community at Louvain, staff and students, were a spiritual elite-in-exile, including philosophers, priest-soldiers, bishops designate. They intended to print spiritual material in Louvain, useful to the Counter Reformation in Ireland, and to publish evidence that would glorify the history of the Irish Church. Its reputation was under serious attack at home and abroad, not only by common propagandists, but by a Scottish theologian, Thomas Dempster, who had kidnapped the entire canon of Irish saints in a semantic raid. Dempster claimed as Scottish every saint to whose name the adjective *Scotus* had ever been appended. The coup included figures as thoroughly green as St Brigid – for *Scotus* of course had traditionally meant Irish. This was a major crisis at the time. Damage to Ireland's religious image would also erode the country's political status in Catholic Europe.

In Louvain, the campaign for the repatriation of the Irish saints was managed primarily by Fathers Hugh Ward and Patrick Fleming. Ward, a young Donegal man, was terminally ill, while Fleming was soon to be murdered in a forest outside Prague, at the age of thirty-two. They were engaged in an emergency attempt to compile 'Lives' of the saints that would lodge them convincingly in the Irish Church.

Michael O'Clery was making a name for himself in Louvain as an historian. In summer 1626, at the instigation of Fr Fleming, he sailed to Ireland to rescue the saints, on a mission that was to last a decade, escalating into a salvage attempt on the entire identity of the Gaelic people.

 # TO DONEGAL

Sailing from Dunkirk, O'Clery may well have travelled up the North Sea, around the tip of Scotland, to reach Donegal, rather than taking the direct route through the English Channel to the south of Ireland. The Hebridean route to and from Europe was normal in times of turmoil. However, with the coronation of Charles I, the oppression of Catholics in Ireland had eased briefly. O'Clery's journey home might be compared to the return of a Buddhist monk into Chinese-occupied Tibet today, on a spiritual mission.

The Franciscan Abbey of Donegal, traditional home of his Order, had been destroyed for a generation or more. The impressive ruins, marred by modern development, overlook the sea on a headland outside Donegal town. The few remaining Franciscans were living in a makeshift settlement at Bundrowes, near Lough Melvin, on the border between Donegal and Leitrim. There is an attractive sculpture in

❧ *Clerical Detective*

Brother Michael's travels throughout seventeenth-century Ireland were traced three hundred years later by Fr Brendan Jennings OFM, in a brilliant analysis of the references, comments, locations and dates jotted on the manuscripts O'Clery produced. A linear pattern, however ghostly, emerged. Jennings' commentary on the story expresses the fervent mentality of a 1930s Ireland which assumed itself to be a direct resumption of the country of the Four Masters. Despite its ardent piety, the research is invaluable and anyone interested in the subject will be deeply indebted to Fr Jennings. The key points of O'Clery's journeys are identified, and sometimes even the texts he transcribed in each location. There is a sense, too, of how those books fitted into the overall pattern of the works produced by O'Clery in rapid succession.

memory of O'Clery and his associates on a minor road-bridge crossing the River Drowes.[1]

There are very few references by contemporary observers of O'Clery's travels. This obscurity is part of his mystique. He was the perfect researcher, his own shadow rarely falling on the work, except as an occasional note on his transcription: – *atú tuirseach gan amhrus. Ag Drobhaois, 3 Marta, 1629.* I'm tired, without doubt. Drowes, 3 March 1629. In one irritable note, he blames the absurdity of a source on the diligence of his superiors who had ordered him to collect absolutely everything.

However, the image of the faceless scholar scurrying from parchment to parchment, shuffling the dry leaves of history, is belied by the brilliance with which he builds his researches into a series of books, culminating in the massive Annals of the Four Masters, requiring the continued presence in a remote location of a team of Ireland's leading bardic historians, supervised by him, all equipped with their ancestral books, and bristling perhaps with allegiances to variants of the past. They had to be funded, fed and accommodated in the wild, their prejudices reconciled. He seems to have prevailed on these scholars to work night and day in what can only have been practical harmony given the amounts of work achieved.

 # DISCREET TRAVEL

Brother Michael is traditionally imagined striding alone throughout Ireland on his journeys of research. The Rule of St Francis advised travel on foot, because the friars and brothers lived by alms and should not be seen to get above themselves. But it seems that Franciscans going on long journeys often rode horses for practical reasons, such as the appalling condition of the tracks that passed as roads. There were times, too, when the number of manuscripts Brother Michael carried with him would have made walking unlikely, such as his final journey, when he is thought to have been burdened with one of the bulkiest texts in the country at the time – whether or not this was actually so. Clearly, he linked together a network of religious establishments and other 'safe houses' on his journeys. A horse and a guide might be available for the next stage. A servant or a lay brother would make a handy porter. The family homes of Franciscans and of others in exile may have provided part of such a system, but no one was keeping a Visitors' Book.

It feels natural to imagine O'Clery travelling swiftly and in silence; not so much heedless of the weather as inured to it, eating sparingly and sleeping on a straw pallet in a monastic dormitory. If he were in any way striking or self-indulgent, given to carousing in alehouses at night, a hint at least would have come down to us in folklore. There is no hint of any kind – not even a tradition of cunning speech, river-leaping, or shape-changing to avoid arrest, as might have been expected of a man of half his achievements. Brother Michael was simply invisible – not just to spies, but to folklore, the most prurient eye of all. Of Geoffrey Keating (Seathrún Céitinn) who was also copying manuscripts at the time, there are intricate myths; these include death at a mass rock, shot by a soldier who was a lapsed Catholic and could see through his invisibility. Of Michael O'Clery, there is hardly a whisper. His death in Louvain in his early fifties tells us, by default, a little about the hardship of his life, the weather, the hunger and the daily rigours of his travels. On the other hand, life-expectancy four hundred years ago hardly extended beyond that.

DUBLIN

His first local journey was from Donegal to Dublin. The Franciscans kept a house in Cook Street, just south of the river behind Merchant's Quay, and he could move discreetly in and out of the city in 1627, engaged in religious research. Such freedom would soon come to an end.[2]

O'Clery had access in Dublin to the library of the Protestant Primate, James Ussher, who owned ten thousand volumes, including rare Irish manuscripts. Ussher was the scholar who traced the Creation of the world to 23 October 4004 BC, thus inaugurating, in the words of a modern historian, 'the practice among Irish antiquarians of showing scant respect for time'.[3]

❧ *Crackdown*

Less than three years after O'Clery's first visit, an order would be issued for the arrest of priests and the suppression of religious houses in Dublin, where large congregations had been attending Masses. The Franciscan house in Cook Street was attacked as Mass was being said on St Stephen's Day 1629. The raid was led by the mayor and the Protestant archbishop of Dublin (not Ussher who was archbishop of Armagh). The mayor damaged some pictures, and the archbishop attacked the pulpit. Uproar broke out. The congregation resisted the attack, and some women rescued two young Franciscan friars who had been arrested. The officials fled, pelted with stones by the crowd. Although the mayor was to become extremely unpopular as a result, the house in Cook Street was demolished. Jesuit houses in Back Lane and Bridge Street were confiscated, and many religious houses throughout the country were suppressed, and in some cases destroyed.

Whether he was assessing the amount of material Ussher had, or whether the library had already been scoured for fugitive saints, Michael O'Clery spent no more than a week in Dublin. Presumably he dressed in secular clothes without distinction. He certainly did not move around town in a long brown robe and sandals, with a cord around his waist and his hair in a Franciscan tonsure. Glancing around the National Library today, over a rampart of O'Clery's Annals, it is tempting to imagine him as pale faced, lightly bearded, thin haired, with a tendency towards dandruff; a little stooped perhaps, and with that inner focus in the eye that responds to print rather that to human intercourse. But this is to forget the outdoor implications of his nickname, Tadhg an tSléibhe. Considering too the project he was to mastermind, he must have had authority, force of will, and above all, endurance. In fact, it is difficult to place him in a library at all.

❋ TORN PAGES

O'Clery moved on from Dublin to Drogheda, where he stayed in a Franciscan house, or a convent as they were often called. It had recently been re-established there, along with a school for religious teaching. These would soon be closed down after the demolition of the house in Cook Street. A chunk from a copy of the Book of Leinster was sent after him from Dublin to Drogheda, and he copied material from it, as he recorded in a note:

> ...*as bloidh do sheinliubhar tainic a hÁth Cliath don Droichet do sccríobadh, 6 Auguist, 1627.*

The habit of giving dates in English, which is noticeable in Donegal Irish today, has a long tradition.

Ten leaves from this actual book, itself a copy, were sent on to Louvain afterwards, where such treasures were being collected. Does this mean that Brother Michael was tearing pages out of books? Unlikely, though he must have been tempted. It is difficult not to be reminded of the Buddhist manuscripts and ancient texts that leaked their way out of Tibet as the Chinese Revolution was burning its way across the country. Some went abroad for safekeeping to the equivalent of Louvain. Many others were sold or destroyed. Curiously, ten vellum pages of the original Book of Leinster are held today in the Franciscan Library, in Killiney, Co. Dublin, while the rest are in Trinity College. Ten pages seems to be the Franciscan share.

It was probably at that point that O'Clery darted across to Kildare, where he copied an ancient text known as the Martyrology of Tallaght, a calendar of Saints' Days dating from the ninth century. Much of the original text is now missing but the blanks have been filled in from his transcription. There are other instances in which his copies provide the contents of lost material. The Annals themselves draw on four texts which would otherwise be completely lost.

Bundrowes

Returning to base, he worked there for the winter on the material he had gathered. Presumably he had other duties as a lay brother in the community, wherever its cluster of thatched huts lurked among the woods and the swampy ground about Lough Melvin. His older brother, Bernardinus, was appointed head of that community and he undoubtedly recognised the importance of the scribal work, since he remained in charge till the very end. In fact, it is possible that the entire structure there was designed to further the Louvain project.

Bundrowes, a ford on the River Drowes, a little south of Bundoran, had always been a noted crossing point, a narrow funnel between Sligo and Donegal. Although Irish monasteries throughout history had occupied such focal points in the landscape, it is unlikely that the Donegal Franciscans in the late 1620s were jumping up and down to attract English attention. The native Irish in the area were remnants of MacClancy's people, described forty years before, by Francisco de Cuéllar with amiable intent as 'savages'. There must have been people within a stone's throw of Michael O'Clery who remembered the Spaniards and even de Cuéllar himself. Sadly, the entire Armada is reduced in the Annals of the Four Masters to fifteen lines of distant and impersonal description, and there is nothing to counterpoint de Cuéllar's famous letter.

✺ HOLY FICTIONS

O'Clery was on the road again in late February 1628, when he stayed in a Franciscan house in Athlone, before making his roundabout way to Dublin for a second visit. It is delicately hinted by scholars that the Latin transcriptions he made in Dublin in July are poor. This might be superiority on the part of commentators who never ate fewer than three meals a day themselves. On the other hand, it might be true, in which case we can sympathise with Michael O'Clery and even grow fond of him.

Whatever about his classical education, Brother Michael was smart enough to know the difficulty of his task and to re-alise his own limitations. He acknowledged that he intended to visit a leading scholar in Tipperary to get help with the difficult parts of *Cáin Adamnáin*, an ancient text which ex-empts women from war and deals with offences such as rape. This set of seventh-century laws also deals with the treat-ment of non-combatants, such as children and priests.

Despite his fidelity to Louvain, he seems to have had his suspicions about hagiography – the literature of the lives of saints. He has been mocked for giving credence to absurdi-ties such as floating stones and a saint aged four hundred and thirteen, but it is easy to understand his being numbed by anachronism as he struggled in a flood of holy fictions.

From Dublin, he travelled southeast in autumn, through Wicklow and Carlow, and across to Cashel in Tipperary. His research in Wicklow has always carried a puzzling hint of scandal because of a note he jotted down in relation to some poems copied at Castlekevin, near Glendalough.[4]

O'Clery referred to the poems as *salach*, dirty. 'The poems

are dirty, though I'm ashamed to admit it for my own part.'
Fr Brendan Jennings translates *salach* as 'disgusting', raising
the odds a lot higher. In fact, when the effort is made to dig
out the offending lines about St Kevin, nothing offensive can
be found in them, apart from a sentimental banality that sits
comfortably in the context of popular verse. Maybe O'Clery
was deploring the text as corrupt, in the sense of diluted or
spoiled. On the other hand, considering the enduring tradition of St Kevin as a misogynist besieged by women, perhaps
O'Clery came across something extra that he did not share.

 # SAINT-COLLECTORS

In Cashel, late that autumn, copiously copying, O'Clery was
among friends or at least fellow spirits. The guardian of the
Franciscan house there was also a saint-collector, while a third
researcher, an undercover priest, remarked in a letter to Louvain that he had met Brother Michael in Cashel where he had
made 'a collection of more than three or four hundred Lives ....'
Difficult times, of course, encouraged anonymity, and the
priest did not make a verbal sketch of O'Clery, who remains as
faceless as the saints whose lives he was recording. Most of
these were no more than names and dates, like a collection of
moths that has withered to dust, leaving pages of scribbles and
rusty pins. These saints continued to haunt the spiritual skies
until the 1960s when the Vatican shot them down in droves.

❋ SCHOLARS

While in Tipperary, O'Clery visited Flann MacEgan, a leading member of the MacAodhagáin family of historians, law-
yers and bards who kept specialised schools in various parts
of the country. O'Clery and his cousin Lughaidh were
trained by Baothgalach MacAodhagáin near Loughrea in Co.
Galway. Flann, the senior historian of this learned family,
lived in north Tipperary, and O'Clery was to visit him several
times throughout the ensuing decade, bringing completed
works for approval. The perilous prospects for Gaelic culture
must have been a constant theme in MacEgan's house. It
seems likely that the ever-ascending spiral of projects that
O'Clery undertook in rapid succession was in some sense
prompted by this centre of learning. O'Clery's work was to
open out far beyond the narrow spiritual focus set by the
authorities at Louvain, to encompass the full potential of the
traditional disciplines in which he had been trained, including history, genealogy and bardic learning.

❋ DONEGAL

Back in Bundrowes for the winter, he tackled the haul of
saints, sorting them into a catalogue of native specimens. No
foreigners were allowed, which might have posed a problem
with St Patrick, but did not. The collection was known as *Fé-
lire na Naomh nErennach* (Calendar of the Irish Saints), now
known as the *Martyrology of Donegal*. The compilation required a great deal of work throughout the winter months,
when conditions were cold by day and smoky by night. Ru-
mours that he had the assistance of the other three masters

❧ Martyrs

A detailed list of Irish martyrs, mostly priests and brothers, killed in Ireland 1565–1655, circulates today on the Internet. It includes hanging, disembowelment, and crushing of the skull, and there is even a priest sold into slavery in 1653. Evidence is lacking, and in some ways these reports are recurring versions of the Martyrologies of the early Christian Church. There are people who believe all of it and people who believe none. The claims are often dismissed as propagandist fabrications. But one has only to look at unstable regimes today to know that state brutality regularly occurs. It is never officially recorded and is always denied. There are Franciscans all over the world today whose lives are under constant threat from military gangs because they are pursuing social justice on behalf of indigenous people. Only the vigilance of the outside world protects them.

Within two years of the completion of O'Clery's book of saints, his superior in Louvain, Fr Fleming, was killed near Prague, where the Franciscans had opened a new college. He was reported to have been hacked to death, at the age of thirty-two, by heretical peasants with axes, while his companion, Father Hore, was nailed to a tree, shot in the breast and had his side pierced by a sword. The account comes from a report in Ó Bruaideadha's *Propugnaculum Catholicae Veritatis*, published in Prague, 1669. (Again, the question of distortion for propaganda purposes arises.) The blissful response of Fr Brendan Jennings OFM, writing in the 1930s, reveals the attitude to such horrors that still existed in a relatively modern Ireland, saturated in the cult of martyrdom. 'Father Fleming,' according to Jennings, 'would scarcely have asked of his beloved Irish saints a more glorious end to the life he had dedicated to their service.'

at this early stage are fanciful. There is a desire among admirers to have them permanently in harness, toiling away by candlelight for the sake of Ireland and the greater glory of God, as if such an image would show the purity of our cause and prove our superiority as a race.

It is difficult to believe that, as a scholar, O'Clery trusted the kind of information he was recording, however strong his faith. The lives of saints are full of transparent contradictions and of oddities passed off as miracles. No wonder he left notes such as, *atu tuirseach gion gub iongnadh* (I'm weary and no wonder). One suspects that the medium itself – the manuscripts, the vellum, the genealogies – *was* history to its keepers, just as the Bible actually *is* religion to some believers. The book, or the bardic poem, was in a sense the real thing, rather than the shadowy people or events that lay behind it.

Michael O'Clery must have been conscious of the danger of his work and his travels in troubled times, although extraordinary reports of freedom in the 1620s abound. One account from Derry asserts that the sheriff heard cases brought by priests against members of their flocks for non-payment of dues, and found in favour of the priests. However, not much more than a generation earlier, the superior of the Franciscans in Donegal, Thaddeus Boyle, had been butchered in the porch of his Abbey, which was eventually destroyed. In 1612, an eighty-year-old Franciscan bishop, Conor O Devaney, was hanged in Dublin, after a jury with only one Irish member found him guilty of treason.

Despite the completion of the Martyrology, O'Clery was on the road again the following summer, zigzagging throughout the south on a mopping-up operation towards a second version of the work. He swept from Cork to Limerick, to Killaloe in Co. Clare, and north to Galway, then back southeast to scoop up crumbs in Clonmel and Wexford. He was driven perhaps to greater urgency by the stabs of futility he experienced. One work he copied in passing was corrupt and uneven, and a great deal of it was utter nonsense, he complained.

It would be wrong to assume that he was concentrating only on saints. Skidding at speed from source to source, he was becoming aware of the range of material available for more pressing work. His reception throughout the country, however muted, was in the tradition of the *aes dána* – the professional intellectuals and craftsmen who had always travelled freely and were welcomed in each others' houses. He had impeccable credentials as a member of the Ó Cléirigh family of historians; as a Franciscan, he encountered a further network of hospitality, tenuous though it must have been.

Back in Bundrowes for another winter, O'Clery further refined the Martyrology, producing a copy for Louvain which was rapturously received by his superiors as the last word in the hagiographical war. They did not see the fretful note jotted down elsewhere: 'And without doubt I recognise that I am writing a great deal slowly, tediously, badly ....' It went on: 'however let the blame be on those people who instructed me to follow the trail of the old books until the time of their revision.' Unfortunately Brother Michael never saw the fruit of his tedious labour published. The Martyrology lay in dusty oblivion for two hundred years and more before it finally reached the public.

O'Clery embarked at once on a more ambitious project; he had not yet shaken off those saints. The Succession of the Kings of Ireland, *Réim Rioghraidhe na hÉireann* and the Genealogies of the Irish Saints, *Seanchas na Naomh* were still related to the original task imposed by Louvain. As Brendan Jennings OFM remarks, a great many holy men were of

❧ *The Competition*

Seathrún Céitinn (Fr Geoffrey Keating), who was collecting material for a history at the same time, was not made as welcome as O'Clery. His ancestors had come to Ireland in the wake of the Anglo-Normans four centuries earlier and, as far as certain learned families in the west were concerned, Keating was not yet out of quarantine. Their suspicions were based on conservatism, but also on the amount of abuse that had been slung at the native Irish by propagandists such as Camden, Campion, Davies, Moryson, Spenser and Stanyhurst. Ironically, one of the main purposes of Keating's work (*Foras Feasa ar Éirinn*) was to refute those distortions, and his work was to be popular for centuries. It was written in a clear, lucid style that anticipated the Irish written today, while O'Clery clung to the archaic language of the bardic classes. It is tempting to imagine O'Clery and Keating tussling over a manuscript in some damp stone house in the early seventeenth century, or removing key material to foil each other, as students did in the UCD library in the 1960s before exams, when crucial texts were rare. But there is no record that O'Clery and Keating ever met, and folklore has not risen to the challenge. O'Clery was to issue a warning later against those with lower standards working in his field, but there was no reason for Keating's ear to itch.

aristocratic stock and so 'it was important to the Irish to trace their lineage, since the Irish always held pedigree in high regard.' In fact, to be brutally honest, the Irish held very little in higher regard than pedigree, and speaking of the Gaelic nobles, it could easily appear that they held nothing in high regard *except* pedigree.

Below the ranks of nobles, senior churchmen and bards, the common people did not officially exist. Pedigree was everything, and genealogy was its science. In the broader sense, genealogy confirmed a solid origin-myth, plugging the race securely back into the generator of the Bible, so that a king or a saint might have his power traced all the way back to Noah.

THE FOUR MASTERS

For this major undertaking (the genealogies of kings and saints), the collaboration of independent historians was required, to ensure balance. But history was a tight little world, and the available experts were closely related. Brother Michael brought together Cúchoigcríche Ó Cléirigh (his own cousin), Fearfeasa Ó Maolchonaire and Cúchoigcríche Ó Duibhgheanáinn – and the Four Masters were formed. As with many a group, the name came later. O'Clery's three collaborators were lay professionals, requiring payment for their work. Fearfeasa belonged to a learned Roscommon family, and was closely related to the Franciscan (Florence Conry) who founded St Antony's College at Louvain. The Ó Duibhgheannáin were traditional historians from Leitrim serving the Ó Fearghail family of Co. Longford.

The four experts came together in late autumn 1630, in a Franciscan convent on the shores of Lough Ree, near Athlone. With a strong sense of destiny, they began work on the Feast of St Francis, 4 October. Their patron lived nearby. If he forgot his obligations, he could be reminded. There must have been an urgent deadline, because they toiled day and night for an intense month, paring the material O'Clery had gathered down to its genealogical skeleton. The urgency may have owed more to the political situation than to the limits of the patron's purse, since most of the Franciscan houses in Ireland closed that year with several hundred monks going into exile.

The work itself is breathtaking in its detail, and accurate within the historical period when checked against other sources. It sweeps way back behind history, of course, and all the kings of Ireland are traced systematically to their mythic origins, with dates and durations of reign quoted. Because the saints are all descended from kings, they follow in groups of geographical origin, commencing with Adamnan and the saints of Donegal.[5]

With great difficulty, Brother Michael had found a patron. Toirrdhealbhach Mac Cochlain was certainly not a master of Irish himself and had been the first to have an ancient text translated into English for his own use. Even the translator took a swipe at him for that, sneering at those Irish 'who choose rather to put their children to learn English than their own native language.'

Brother Michael was not so arrogant as to insult his patron. In an opening dedication, he made a number of things clear: the Franciscans were subject to oppression; four years had been spent collecting material; many 'honourable gentlemen' not subject to vows of poverty, had refused to fund the compilation. Not so Toirrdhealbhach Mac Cochlain, son of Seamas, son of Seamas, son of Seamas, son of Seamas, son of Toirrdhealbhach, son of Fedlimidh … and so on back through dozens of generations to Míl Espáine (who seeded the Gaelic race in Ireland), and thence step by step to Noah and to Adam. For his sponsorship of the Genealogy, Mac Cochlain was truly rewarded in kind, with his lineage immortalised on the opening page.

On completion, the *Succession of Kings and Saints* was dispatched to Louvain, where it took its place with the earlier work in oblivion for several hundred years.

BOOK OF INVASIONS

Ireland was bleak and dangerous in 1631. Franciscan contacts had fled, and the 'safe houses' had shut down. The fieldwork was suspended. What O'Clery had collected in the previous four years would have to do. For the moment, his travels ceased, although he would take to the road again, a few years later, in a last great sweep throughout the country.

He began his masterwork at the beginning (if not before it), by compiling the legendary history of Ireland from the Creation to the twelfth century AD. This involved a synthesis of all the existing versions of *Lebor Gabála Érenn*, the Book of Invasions, which details the early conquests of the island and the migrations of the would-be Irish from Scythia to Babel, to Egypt at the time of Moses, and finally to Spain, before reaching Ireland as Míl and Sons, around the time of Alexander the Great.

Again, O'Clery brought his collaborators together, having arranged a patron, Brian Roe Maguire, Baron of Enniskillen. The chief chronicler of the Maguires sat in on the process, to protect the patron's interests and to assist. They brought the books of their various families and many other texts to bear on the work. O'Clery added a Preface, in which his pride as a professional finally asserted itself without the standard humility. He said that men less skilled in Irish had been about to undertake the task. Their work would have been 'an eternal reproach and disgrace to all Ireland, and particularly so to her chroniclers ....'

Brother Michael had reverted to Tadhg an tSléibhe Ó Cléirigh, historian to a line of chieftains. Could he have been competing with this threat for several years in advance, knowing that hagiography was keeping him from his real work? The Book of Invasions was completed in eight frantic weeks at the convent of Lisgoole, on the banks of Lough Erne.

 THE ANNALS

A month to the day after finishing it, the experts assembled again – this time at the Franciscan convent of Bundrowes. On 22 January 1632, they commenced the Annals of the Kingdom of Ireland, *Annála Ríoghachta Éireann*. The project – to compile a diary of Ireland's history, from Creation until their own time – took four and a half years to complete, with perhaps two years of full-time work involved. The revised Book of Invasions slotted in at the beginning of the Annals, giving them a head start in prehistory.

The annalists were fed and accommodated at the expense of the Franciscan convent, a major burden in a lean time. Fr Bernardinus O'Clery, Michael's older brother, was superior by then. As if to prove the contemporary appeal of the project, there was again a generous patron – Fergal O'Gara of Sligo. He too has been given the kind of fame that only money can buy. A small-time landowner, he sat as one of the few Gaelic Irish in the Dublin Parliament of 1634. As a ward of the Crown, he had received a Protestant education at Trinity, in an attempt to wean him from his roots. There is a fine irony in his patronage of the Annals, the ultimate affirmation of Gaelic tradition. Perhaps the contradictions in his background should have been seen as a sign of all that Ireland, at its best, would become. But they were not. For centuries, the debate seldom rose above the question of whether O'Gara did, or did not, turn Catholic on his death-bed.

Brother Michael, who is thought to have secured the sponsorship personally, knew the value of it. Without the money, the work would not have been possible. In a dedication to O'Gara he noted, '... should the writing [of the Annals] be neglected at present, they would not again be found to be put on record or commemorated, even to the end of the world.' This pre-echoes Tomás Ó Críomthain's famous conclusion to *An tOileánach* (The Islandman), in which he memorialises his island people in the phrase: ... *mar ní bheidh ár leithéidí ann arís.* (... because our likes will not come again.) The repetition of such a note in major works of Irish literature is ominous, suggesting a raven's quote or a requiem bell at the heart of the culture.

All available texts were brought together at Bundrowes, but the annalists were cut off from southern connections by the political circumstances. The Annals show a heavy dependence on Ulster and Connacht sources. (Of course, there is no guarantee that such an emphasis would have been avoided in better times.) Nevertheless, they linked together a chain of ordered references, detailing the history of Ireland year by year from the coming of Ceasair, forty days before the Flood.[6]

A comparison of all the still-existing sources (four are now lost) with the completed Annals reveals how the annalists worked. They were experts on chronology. They sat around a table with the various books open in their midst. The events of each year, from the beginning of time, were read out from the texts; they were argued, debated, synthesised and compiled into agreed entries. None would have been ready to concede the competing claims of their ancestral books. Their entire existences were predicated on the almost scriptural accuracy of their records. And yet they compressed, selected, double-entered, shifted delicately ... Judging by the variety of handwriting in the Annals, they took it in turns to act as scribes. Among the faults for which they are criticised was the uniform 'house style' they imposed – the stylised language of their trade, which retained none of the original flavour of lost sources.

There is something eerie about their deep and systematic delving into the past at that moment in Irish history, as if they could find some hidden flaw, reconstruct a noble pattern, without reaching a state of exile and dispossession in the present – as if the glory of the written past could exorcise the future threat. But that is to romanticise their motives. Perhaps, for them, the only real future *was* the past. As historians (chroniclers, to be precise) they had an overwhelming obligation to their profession, like astronomers who would examine the stars most keenly during a meltdown of the heavens.

The last words of the Annals (a eulogy for Hugh O'Neill, Earl of Tyrone) were written on Sunday, 10 August 1636. A double-set had been produced – one for O'Gara, one for Louvain. The text was prepared with print in mind, laid out for publication. Michael O'Clery would not see it reach that stage.

CROSS-COUNTRY

Although it was mid-autumn, he set off immediately on a ritual journey throughout Ireland, bringing a copy of the manuscript with him to receive the approval of major scholars and ecclesiastics. It is tempting to imagine him scorching along the familiar roads, shouldering an enormous wedge of text, dumping it in front of startled bishops.

However, the entire manuscript would have been a very bulky load. And if it was one of only two copies, then it was a valuable load indeed, at a dangerous time. Perhaps he brought an edited selection with him rather than an original. He stayed nowhere long enough to have the complete manuscript examined. A benevolent scan and he was gone, in pursuit of the next *imprimatur*. No one complained or found fault. Not yet.

He travelled continuously during that winter, and the work was received everywhere with approval. The principal historians he visited were Flann MacEgan in Tipperary, and Conor MacBrody, just beyond the town of Gort. The visits were brief. No complaint of a northern bias was made.

Next, he went on a galloping tour of the bishops – first to Galway, then to the Bishop of Elphin; from there to Kildare and on to Dublin, where Thomas Fleming, the Franciscan archbishop, signed the manuscript in mid-February. Another of the bishops visited was Baothghalach Mac Aodhagáin, whose school Tadhg an tSléibhe had attended as a student. Afterwards, Brother Michael rejoined the deep rut he had personally worn in the road to Donegal.

BACKLASH

A vicious row broke out almost immediately over the accuracy of the Annals. The complaint was made and circulated, not by any rabid southern poet, but by Tuileagna Ó Maolchonaire, who was not only related to one of the annalists but was a Franciscan himself. To compound the double stab in the back, Tuileagna (flood of knowledge) would later describe himself as historian-general of Ireland. He claimed to have found five major flaws in the Annals. The books, he said, were not read, or were only partly read, in the rush to get signatures. Shouting from the rooftops, he asserted that MacBrody and MacEgan, the senior historians, had withdrawn their approval, and he demanded that publication be withheld. If he knew as much of the present as he claimed to know of the past, he would have had the wit to realise that there was little danger of publication.

Tuileagna's five arguments are all noise and no content. Trivial issues of lineage and nomenclature, they sound insane outside the context of their own time. Even then, they must have reeked of bombast and rhetoric. In the fifth argument, he tried to enlist his own province of Connacht on his side, by disputing a claim in the Annals that the O'Donnells of the north had levied rent in Connacht. (They had.) Even if they had levied it in a portion of the province, he argued, that would make the manner of the statement an insult to the whole of Connacht.

RESPONSE

After a delay of several years, Fearfeasa Ó Maolchonaire responded to his kinsman's arguments, on behalf of the annalists. 'To be brief,' he wrote at length, 'as I was unwilling that anyone of the name he bears should be publicly shown to be in manifest error, I told him privately the rights of the case before going to plead it in the presence of the judges.'

They had been summoned before a General Chapter of the Franciscans in Multyfarnham, for adjudication. Tuileagna did not accept the judgement, and his claims were even more loudly discussed than before, 'from mouth to mouth in every part of Ireland'. Fearfeasa said that Brother Michael himself had already answered the objections, but '… as many people are more eager to have error disseminated among them than the truth, the erroneous and bitter statements of Tuileagna are more widely scattered over Ireland than the plain, sensible, dignified and substantial reply to them by the Brother.' Therefore, Fearfeasa was publishing his own response in order to put an end to the 'disgrace, contempt and reproach' which had begun to accrue to the annalists.

Having shafted his opponent from every direction, Fearfeasa then pulled a masterstroke. He announced that he would adhere to the ancient manner and make his rebuttal in bardic verse rather than in prose. From that point on, the issue was incomprehensible. Time stood still. If anything, it went backwards. Eventually, if only for the sake of continuity, the future judged in favour of Brother Michael.

 EXILE

With bitter arguments ringing in his ears and his manuscript under his arm, Brother Michael left Ireland never to return – like many a writer since. He set out by boat from Carrickfergus to Louvain on his last long journey, in July 1637. In his late forties by then, he had been absent for eleven years. He produced one more work: a dictionary of obscure terms in Old Irish, which was published in Louvain in 1643. A key to complex translations, it was the only one of his works to be published in his lifetime. Later that year, in his early fifties, he died and was buried in Louvain without trace.

Michael O'Clery never knew he was chief of 'The Four Masters'. That term was devised by a later generation, recalling a Franciscan tradition of *quattuor magistri*. It is typical of his life that his remains should have disappeared without celebration or trace, although his work has become a byword for the past. To conceive, to set up, and to pursue the work to conclusion was an enormous challenge at a time when resources of all kinds were diminishing. O'Clery's reference to the 'end of the world', a rhetorical flourish in the dedication, caused later generations to believe that Gaelic culture had been on the edge of an abyss then. It was thought that the annalists had recognised the crisis, and that, poised on the lip of the fracture, they had achieved a miraculous act of salvage. Charged with emotion, such beliefs continued to have a symbolic effect for centuries. That effect, however false, was useful to the survival of the culture. Now that the symbolism has become threadbare, a new kind of belief is necessary if survival is to grow into actual recovery – some strange blend of independence and self-confidence perhaps.

END NOTES

INTRODUCTION

1.   Derived from *Brassica*, the Latin term for cabbage, *praiseach* has come to mean a slovenly mess in Irish.

I GREAT ESCAPE

1. Kidnap and Jailbreak: Red Hugh O'Donnell

1.   According to the 'Life' by Ó Cléirigh. The captain is named elsewhere as John Bermingham.

2.   The Rev. Paul Walsh, whose commentary on the 'Life' is responsible for popular opinion on the route, opts lightly for Glenasmole, Lough Bray, Sally Gap, and the Valley of the Annamoe.

3.   The present fourth storey and the battlements were added in 1814.

4.   O'Sullivan's Latin account has *serica tela*, which has been translated as silk coverlets or curtains. Hard to trust the knots in such material.

II SURVIVAL MARCH

2. The Hungry Road: March of O'Sullivan Beare

1.   In O'Sullivan's time, Keimaneigh was a rugged defile, clenched between steep slopes and cliffs, with mountains rising on both sides. To put it behind him on the first day would be a decisive move; he would enter a different region – Muskerry – home of the MacAuliffes, O Keeffes and MacCarthys.

An older route crossed the east shoulder of the pass, without the threat of ambush. O'Sullivan's convoy entered Muskerry late in the day, filing steeply downhill well to the east of Gougane Barra, the great mountain corrie sacred to St Finbarr, where the River Lee rises. They were in a kind of internal exile then. In a country of warlords, garrisons, shifting allegiances, there was no continuous state under their feet when they crossed from one territory to another.

2.   George Carew, Lord President of Munster, had posted a price of £300 on O'Sullivan's head, which must have stirred the bounty hunter in his neighbours.

III POWER-JOURNEYS:
KINGS & QUEENS

4. Medb and the Cattle-raid of Cooley

1.   Fergus mac Róich is a well-known character in the ancient literature, quite apart from the Táin itself. His virility is reported to have been of equine proportions. This explains why he was drafted into the Táin as the story developed: to match the reputation of Queen Medb. At one stage of the Táin journey, King Ailill spies on the entwined lovers. He steals Fergus's sword and has it replaced with a wooden one in a piece of symbolism from comic burlesque.

2.   There were major fords up and down the river, which might have suited better. Further south (near Clonmacnoise), a gravel-ridge cut the Shannon. This was the *Eiscir Riada*, a bank of moraine deposited by receding ice and crossing Ireland from Dublin to Galway. Where it was breached by the river, sections of higher ground remained between the strands of the current, creating a logical ford. The Shannon Commissioners dredged and deepened the main channel in the 1840s, lowering the level of the river in the process.

3.   The culture of Ireland in the Pagan Iron Age is characterised by features recognisable from the European Celts, such as the use of chariots. This culture would reach a climax and then collapse. Its lore and legends would remain fixed at a certain point in time. It was replaced by a later culture whose folk heroes, *na Fianna*, would continue to develop in the imagination right through to modern literature.

4.   Their confinement has been read as a classic case of *couvade*, a common practice of primitive tribes whereby men go into labour and upstage their pregnant women. The practice also occurs in modern culture.

5.   *Dinnseanchas*, the lore of place, was actually responsible. The fact that there was a point on the River Dee with a name that sounded somewhat like *Fear Diadh* allowed a story to develop around a warrior of that name. Being close to the heartland of the Cuchulainn myth, it was logical that the two would then confront each other.

6.   '... *co ndechaid dar timthireacht a chuirp agus gorbo lán cach n-áge de dá fhorrindibh.*'

      '... and it [*ga bolga*] entered his body through the anus and filled every joint and limb of him with its barbs.' *Táin*: transl. Cecile O'Rahilly.

IV THE HALO & THE SWORD

6. Warrior and Saint: Caoilte and St Patrick

1.   Further north, the myth of Cuchulainn shows a similar organic development, as different groups build up a composite hero to symbolise their story.

2.   The exaggerated prowess of Caoilte and his comrades contains a core of truth. Small groups of professional warriors, well-equipped, could always hammer large numbers of unskilled soldiers.

3.   That the saint left his mark on *Cruachain* is also claimed by Tírechán, who described him carrying out baptisms at the Well of *Clébach*, known today as the popular Patrician shrine of Ogulla.

4. In the Early Christian era, most churches were built, not of stone, but of wood and thatch. Masonry was dry stone, severely limited in height. The Romans were using cement in Europe, but the Irish were not impressed. The round tower would not be possible, however, until they accepted mortar.

7. Towards the Annals of the Four Masters:
The Travels of Michael O'Clery

1. The exact location of the settlement has long been a source of heated speculation, as if it might somehow retain an essence of the campaign, but the absolute disappearance of any trace is typical of O'Clery himself and of his reluctance to intrude on the physical record

2. There were reported to be fourteen Catholic churches and eighty priests in Dublin, plus a further three thousand throughout the country. This comes from a Protestant account which complains that the people groaned under the burden of priests. A little earlier, in 1623, the Catholic Archbishop of Dublin estimated eight hundred priests in Ireland. To these he added 'about two hundred Franciscans, who are especially to be recommended because they never suffered themselves to become extinct in the kingdom.'

3. Actually, Ussher was an outstanding scholar, taking to a logical conclusion the dating conventions common to historians at the time, based on genealogy and the Old Testament. Although he was anti-Catholic, he worked closely with Gaelic counterparts on antiquarian research.

4. This was the ancestral home of the O'Tooles, the house Red Hugh O'Donnell reached on his first escape from Dublin (see Chapter 1).

5. A separate entry for St Patrick is worth quoting.
(*m* = mac/son of) Patraicc *m* Calpuirn *m* Fodaighe *m* Oduis *m* Coirniuil *m* Liber *m* Mercuit *m* Oda *m* Oricc *m* Muricc *m* Oircc *m* Leo *m* Maxim *m* Otraicc *m* Erise *m* Peliste *m* Ferine *m* Briotáin *m* Ferghasa leithdercc *m* Nemhidh *m* Agnamain – (who goes straight back to Adam.)

6. The books present were: The Book of Clonmacnoise; The Book of the Island of Saints (Lough Ree); The Book of Seanadh Mic Magnusa in Lough Erne; The Book of Clann Ua Maolchonaire; The Book of Ó Duibhgheanáinn; and The Book of Lecan Mac Firbisigh.

RECOMMENDED READING

Allingham & Crawford, *Captain Cuellar's Adventures*, London, 1897.

An Seabhach P. Ó Siochfhradha, *Laoithe na Féinne*, Dublin, 1941.

Bartlett, Thomas and Jeffery, Keith (eds.), *A Military History of Ireland*, Cambridge University Press, 1996.

Brady, Ciaran, *Shane O'Neill*, Hist. Assoc. of Ireland, 1996.

Dasent, GW (transl. & ed.), *Saga of Burnt Njal*, London, 1861

de Paor, Liam (ed.), *Milestones in Irish History*, Mercier Press, 1986.

Dooley & Roe (transl. & ed.), *Tales of the Elders of Ireland*, Oxford, 1999.

Duffy, Seán (ed.), *Atlas of Irish History*, Gill & Macmillan, 2000.

Dunlevy, Mairéad, *Dress in Ireland: A History*, The Collins Press, 1999.

Flanagan, Laurence, *Irish Wrecks of the Spanish Armada*, Country House, Dublin, 1995.

Forey, P & Fitzsimons, C, *Biaphlandaí*, An Gúm, 1997.

Gallagher, P & Cruicshank, DW (eds.), *God's Obvious Design*, Spanish Armada Papers, Tamesis, London, 1990.

Hannigan, Ken (ed.) & Nolan, William, *Wicklow: History & Society*, Geography Publications, 1994.

Harbison, Peter, *Pilgrimage in Ireland*, Syracuse University Press, 1995.

Jennings, Rev. Brendan, O.F.M., *Mícheál Ó Cléirigh and his Associates*, Talbot Press, 1936.

Kelly, Fergus, *Early Irish Farming*, Dublin Inst. for Advanced Studies, 1997.

Kinsella, Thomas (transl.), *The Táin*, Oxford, 1970.

Lucas, AT, *Cattle in Ancient Ireland*, Boethius Press, Kilkenny, 1989.

Leerssen, Joep, *Mere Irish and Fíor-Ghael*, Cork University Press, 1996.

Malone, JB, *Walking in Wicklow*, Helicon, 1964.

McCarthy, Denis, *Dublin Castle*, Oifig an tSoláthair, 1997.

Mitchell, Frank & Ryan, Michael, *Reading the Irish Landscape*, Town House, 1997.

Morgan, Hiram, *Tyrone's Rebellion*, Gill & Macmillan, 1993.

Newman, Roger Chatterton, *Brian Boru*, Anvil Books, 1987.

Ní Shéaghdha, N (ed.), *Agallamh na Seanórach*, 3 vols, Dublin, 1942–45.7

Nicholls, Kenneth, *Gaelic and Gaelicised Ireland in the Middle Ages*, Gill & Macmillan, 1972.

Nowlan, Kevin B (ed.), *Travel and Transport in Ireland*, Gill & Macmillan, 1993.

Ó Corráin, Donnchadh, *Ireland before the Normans*, Gill & Macmillan, 1972.

O'Donovan, John (transl. & ed.), *Annals of the Four Masters*, Dublin, 1851.

O'Grady (transl. & ed.), *Agallamh na Senórach*, Silva Gadelica, London, 1892.

Ó hÓgáin, Daithí, *Myth, Legend and Romance*, Prentice Hall Press, 1991.

O'Rahilly, Cecile (transl. & ed.), *Táin Bó Cúalnge*, Dublin Inst. for Advanced Studies.

O'Sullivan, Philip, *Historiae Catholicae Iberniae Compendium* Byrne, Sealy, etc. Dublin, 1903

Ó Tuama, Seán, *Repossessions*, Cork University Press, 1995.

Smyth, AP, *Celtic Leinster*, Irish Academic Press, 1982.

Somerville-Large, Peter, *From Bantry to Leitrim*, Gollancz, 1974.

Stafford, Thomas, *Pacata Hibernia*, Downey & Co., London, 1896.

Todd, JH (ed.), *Cogadh Gaedhel re Gallaibh*, London, 1867.

Walsh, Paul, Rev. (ed.), *Beatha Aodha Ruaidh Uí Dhomhnaill*, Irish Texts Society, 1948.

Walsh, Paul, Rev., *The Ó Cléirigh Family of Tír Conaill*, Dublin, 1938.